YELLOW LEAF

YELLOW LEAF

MARY JOYCE CAPPS

ILLUSTRATED BY DON KUEKER

Publishing House
St. Louis   London

Concordia Publishing House, St. Louis, Missouri
Concordia Publishing House Ltd., London, E. C. 1
Copyright © 1974 Concordia Publishing House
Library of Congress Catalog Card No. 73-11874

ISBN 0-570-03603-8

MANUFACTURED IN THE UNITED STATES OF AMERICA

To my father
Arthur C. Ragan Sr.
Yellow Leaf's grandson

CHAPTER 1

The big man's shoulders slumped with fatigue as he dismounted and led his horse into the clearing. He untied a rope, tethered a heavily laden pack mule to a limb, and unloaded heavy traps. As he tended the animals and moved about the campsite, he was not aware that dark eyes watched every move.

His breath made steamy puffs in the crisp pine-scented air. The temperature had dropped sharply since morning. It was late autumn, but the trees were stubbornly holding onto their colorful leaves. His intuition warned that the coming winter was going to be a bad one. But it would be good for trapping, and the fur would be prime. Now that he had selected this place, he hoped the snows would wait until he had built a small cabin and a shelter for the horse and mule.

The white man hunkered over a cooking fire. His face was ruddy in reflected light from the dancing flames. A few unruly gray curls had escaped the front of his red wool cap and were plastered to his forehead by perspiration. Suddenly he froze and stopped stirring the food as a prickle of dread rippled up his back. Without raising his head, his eyes darted around the clearing. The danger he sensed must be behind him! Grabbing up his rifle, he whirled to confront it.

His fears were not allayed as he saw the tiny Indian girl who silently stared him down with large black eyes.

She was only a mite of a thing. About three years old, he would guess, and Cherokee, from her dress. Where were her people? How many were there? Were they friendly?

The white man slipped into the dark forest and searched a wide area before circling back to his camp, thoroughly perplexed. He and the child were apparently the sole occupants of the area. Yet it wasn't possible. "Injuns jest don't dump their younguns and go skitterin' off," he muttered uneasily.

He returned to find the girl seated cross-legged by the fire, scraping the bottom of the cooking pot. "You're a'polishin' off my supper," he growled. She wasn't frightened. She rose and gravely handed him the empty pan. "Et every bite of it, you did," he accused bitterly, turning the pot over the flames to clean it. He was too tired to prepare more food. He felt angry and overwhelmed by unwanted responsibility as he saw the child curl up near the fire and fall asleep. "You kin stay 'til mornin', but that's all!" he muttered, covering her with a warm wolf pelt. "And I hope yer folks will understand I didn't kidnap you — didn't want no part of you, in fact!"

After he had searched for three days — wasted days, needed for building a cabin — the trapper gave up. Like it or not, he was stuck with the girl until someone showed up to claim her.

Even if she spoke his language, the child couldn't have explained that this wasn't likely to happen. Her tribe had been uprooted from their ancestral home in the Great Smoky Mountains and forced off their land, several hundred miles east of here. They had only passed through the area on their unhappy way to the Indian Territory.

Not even the adult Indians fully understood why an army of 7,000 white soldiers was driving them like cattle toward desolate flat lands far to the west. Some 17,000 of the girl's people had been rounded up, intimidated and robbed of their possessions, then placed in concentration camps. Mothers were often separated from their children in the terrible confusion. Tears gushed down the faces of strong warriors as they watched.

During the terrible yearlong "death march" that the Indians called Nanna-da-ul-tsun-yi, "Trail where they cried," over 4,000 men, women, and children perished from the cold and hardships. Many others were never reunited with their families.

The Indians were meat eaters, suddenly disarmed and not allowed to hunt for food as they traveled. Only the strongest could stomach the grain and other scant food the soldiers fed them. Hungry, the child had wandered away into the forest. It happened often with the young, and the very old, who deliberately went away to die. There had already been cold fall rains, sleet, and light snows. What was to be a bitter winter was coming, and they had hundreds of miles to travel. The long march could not be delayed to search for another lost child—who was probably already dead. Face haunted by his distasteful assignment, the young army officer grimly signaled the start of another day's march, trying not to hear the keening wails of a frantic young mother. Would he ever sleep untroubled again, he wondered.

Cagle was the only name the white man had, for he knew as little about his family as the girl could tell about hers. He had been an orphan and on his own as far back as he could remember. Casting about for a name for his unwanted charge, he was awed as a single golden leaf released its hold on a branch, fluttered down, and stuck in her black hair. "Yellow Leaf! It sounds Injun, and besides, I guess one name's as good as another," he told the solemn child.

Watching Yellow Leaf as he rested beside the half-finished cabin, Cagle began to understand how the girl had survived. How long he could only guess. Having known many Indians, the trapper still marveled at her independence and wondered if the child really needed him. She was less trouble than he had expected. The Indians' habits, customs, and beliefs were so deeply entwined with the earth and nature that they, and Yellow Leaf, were born with instincts essential to survive. Alone, if necessary.

She often drifted away, then returned eating a bird's egg from an abandoned nest. Sometimes she preferred bark or moss to the food he prepared, or nibbled contentedly on delicate ferns. "I guess it's all right as long as you don't pizon yerself," he muttered, as he set back to work. Since there would be two of them wintering here, he had decided to make the cabin larger, which would take longer.

When they were moved in and his traps set in the first deep snow, Cagle shaved pelts with his skinning knife and awkwardly fashioned warmer clothes for Yellow Leaf. He used narrow strips of hide to lace the seams together. The girl seemed pleased with her crude outfit and stood quietly as he trimmed the fringe on the too-long skirt. But he ran into trouble when he remarked that the necklaces dangling around her neck made her look like a heathen and attempted to remove them.

"No, Cagle! No! No! No!" she shrieked fiercely. She sank her teeth into his thumb and pummeled him with tiny clenched fists.

The surprised trapper retreated to the split log table, sat down, and glared at her. "Yo're a savage, that's whut you are! And sneaky, too. How long you been understandin' all the talkin' I do to myself?"

10

"Cagle, Cagle, Cagle," she retorted softly. She picked up his hand and rubbed her cheek against the calloused palm.

It was the first such sign of emotion he had seen out of the child, who was stoic and proud; always silent and self-contained. Something about her action reminded him of wolves. Once their terrible fighting was over, he had seen the magnificent animals creep on their bellies to a newly victorious leader and, one by one, lower their massive heads to the ground. Apparently a sign of respect and loyalty.

With awkward gentleness the trapper gathered her into his lap and stroked her long hair. She smiled up at him adoringly and snuggled close. They were friends.

Yellow Leaf grew plump and dimpled during the winter. It was a pleasure to watch her tumble and play like a kitten on the fur rug in front of the fireplace. She was a natural mimic. Sometimes she put on Cagle's heavy boots and crushed his battered summer hat down on her head and wobbled across the floor like a drunk. She giggled breathlessly and Cagle roared with laughter when the boot laces tangled and threw her to the floor. She needed toys to play with.

One day Cagle found a cedar tree, split and burned from a lightning strike. Among the fragments was a small rounded piece of wood. He carried it home and whittled off the jagged edges on one side. Then he carved out a crude face and used a piece of fur to make hair. He selected a thick chunk of firewood for the body, wrapped it in a strip of blanket, and laced it tight with thongs.

"Makin' a doll is one of the last things I ever expected to be doin'," Cagle remarked, as his large fingers struggled with knots. "And you prob'ly won't even know what it is anyway."

11

The girl sat across from him and watched intently as he fought to assemble the pieces. Her head was barely above the tabletop. Her jet black eyes reflected wonder when Cagle offered it to her. "It's yours. It's a doll baby. Go on, take it," he urged. Curious, she prodded the blanket body with one finger, but made no attempt to hold it. Delight and understanding swept over her dusky face when the big man awkwardly cradled the doll in his arms and rocked it.

"Kick . . . Kick," Yellow Leaf murmured. She took the doll and clasped it to her bosom. Cagle was familiar with the word. It meant mother. The big man's eyes stung as he saw the sudden yearning look on the girl's face. She laid her cheek against the small head. "Ah, well. Maybe I shouldn't have made it," he sighed, touching her cheek. "All I done was bring back sad memories fer you."

Yellow Leaf sensed his disappointment. Eyes soft with love, she put her hand over his for a moment before she carried the doll to the fireplace and sat down. Cagle felt moved and suddenly alone. A gentle smile played around Yellow Leaf's mouth as she rocked and chanted a lullaby he couldn't understand to the bundle of wood and cloth. She seemed lost from him. What or whom did she see in the dancing flames? His cabin was haunted by the girl's unknown mother. "And mine too," the trapper thought. He rose quickly and swept the wood shavings and scraps of cloth off the table. The child could raise such storms of emotion within him and remind him of things forgotten so long ago.

The doll was really a farewell gift. The snow was melting rapidly; tall brown weeds and stalks already poked through in places. Yesterday Yellow Leaf had found green ferns snuggled on the protected side of a rotting log. It had been a long time since they had eaten greens. The girl pounced on them and popped a frond in her mouth. She plucked others to share with him. Cagle hoped he could trust her judgment as he gingerly accepted the small wad she handed to him. They tasted better than he expected, although he didn't enjoy them as much as she did.

Later, when Yellow Leaf was asleep, the doll still clasped in her arms, Cagle stared down at her. How tempted he was to keep her instead of taking her to the Indian camp that would soon appear at the river. He planned now to spend another winter or two here before moving on. Those first few weeks he would have given the girl to almost anyone. He bitterly resented her. He had always been alone and thought he was probably as happy as most other men. Now it would be like leaving a part of himself. Which was all the more reason, he had decided, to do it before he got even more attached to the child. She was Indian and would never be accepted by whites. He had to return her to her own people. His face bleak, Cagle sifted ashes over dying embers and prepared for bed.

CHAPTER 2

During the next three weeks the trapper worked feverishly as he made preparations to leave the cabin until next fall. He would sell his pelts and then find a job on a farm or take a flatboat trip downriver. He brought in the traps and stored them. Yellow Leaf was excited by all the unaccustomed activity. It was different from the leisurely pace of their winter days. She followed him along the traplines and around the yard, the doll cradled in her arms. Her sturdy brown legs raced to keep up with Cagle's long strides. He had everything ready now; they could leave the cabin at sunup. Yellow Leaf didn't notice the pain that crossed his face when she clutched his hand and skipped along beside him.

They traveled all day. There were no men in sight when Cagle rode his tired horse into the Indian settlement. They were evidently hunting or away trading the winter's furs for supplies. He led the mule, piled high with his own pelts. A group of young boys were shooting arrows with amazing accuracy at a small scrap of hide nailed to a tree. A pack of dogs rushed the intruders, then stopped barking and slunk away when an older youth shouted. Women and girls who were grinding corn or cooking outside the tepees stopped working. Others who were washing clothing in the river also quit their work. No warning was given, but all the young girls vanished into the tepees or melted away into the forest.

The older women grouped together and watched warily as Cagle dismounted. "Does anyone here speak English?" the trapper asked. An infant wailed and was quieted by its mother. No one answered but an elderly woman moved forward, slightly ahead of the others. Cagle sighed. Sign language was slow and difficult. How could he ever explain about Yellow Leaf, or that he needed to find a family to take her?

Cagle pointed to the furs, then to himself. The woman nodded. She already knew the white man was a trapper. A fleeting smile crossed her face as he reached up and lifted Yellow Leaf down. The child stuck a finger in her mouth and clung to the man's leg as she watched the women. Her eyes were large and frightened. The child's obvious trust in the man told the Indian woman what she wanted to know. He was a good man who had been kind to the small Indian girl. Turning, she motioned to the older boy who had called off the dogs.

"I can understand and speak with you," the youth said slowly. He frowned and flushed when the small crowd of boys broke into giggles at his strange sounding words. A scornful glance from the woman silenced them. She spoke to one of the other women who quickly spread a buffalo robe on the cold ground beside a cooking fire. The boy sat down on one side and motioned for Cagle to be seated on the other. Never letting go of him, Yellow Leaf snuggled against his side, eyes alert and watchful.

Leaving her was so painful that Cagle wanted to explain about her very quickly, then ride his horse away. But this was not the Indian way. Because of the girl, one of their own race, he deserved different treatment than would be accorded any other white man who entered their village while the men were away. First they would eat, Cagle and the youth, then they would talk. The trapper waited, trying to be patient, as steaming bowls of meat and vegetables were brought to them. Yellow Leaf refused to be drawn away from him and the women looked shocked when he began to feed her from his bowl.

Cagle didn't notice. He had no way of knowing they were displaying bad manners. According to their custom, women and children should not eat until the men have finished. The waiting showed respect for braves, who, after all, provide food for their families. Nevertheless, Yellow Leaf was hungry after the long hours of riding and the trapper was less concerned about his own hunger. The Indians were too polite to point out his breach of etiquette, but they felt ashamed that an Indian girl would eat so ravenously instead of coming to stand with them and wait.

As the youth laid aside his bowl and waited expectantly, the women crowded closer, but none of them sat down. Cagle spoke slowly and clearly. He didn't want to have to repeat. All he wanted was to have done with it and leave quickly. The boy had introduced himself as Black Bear, the son of their chief. The older woman was his mother, Grazing Fawn. He listened to the trapper carefully, then translated. Anxious, Cagle watched the woman's face. Her son was too young to be a brave; Grazing Fawn would make the final decision. The tribe was small. Yellow Leaf would be another mouth to feed. Suppose they refused to take her!

The air was cold but a sheen of perspiration glistened on the trapper's forehead as the boy and his mother talked back and forth. It was taking so long! Cagle could understand a few words, but not enough to know how the decision would go.

"My mother has no daughter. The girl has no manners

and has much to learn. She says she will keep your Yellow Leaf," the youth finally told Cagle.

The trapper nodded bleakly, almost wishing she had refused. He picked up her small sturdy hand and slowly led Yellow Leaf to the woman. "I can't take you with me. I'm white, and yo're Indian. You have to stay here with this woman. These here are yer people," he said. He strode to the mule, removed three pelts, and handed them to Black Bear. "These beaver skins will help pay her keep," he mumbled. Cagle mounted the horse and turned it. "I won't look back," he gritted, "but the Lord help me make it to them trees before she starts cryin' after me!" Yellow Leaf seldom cried, but he always melted if she did.

Yellow Leaf didn't cry as she watched him ride away. She was bewildered and a little frightened at being left with strangers, but she trusted Cagle. He had to leave her for a while but she never doubted that he would return for her.

Grazing Fawn had seen the pain in the white man's eyes, so she too expected to see him again. There was too strong a bond of love between the two. She grew to love Yellow Leaf, but she constantly reminded herself that having her was probably only temporary. The child was obedient, but she sat for hours holding the doll Cagle had made for her and watching the trail that led into the village. She obviously considered herself only a visitor here.

Thus the Indian woman was not surprised when the trapper revisited their camp in the fall. His mule was laden with food and supplies for the winter. The excited Yellow Leaf launched herself at him like a small whirlwind. Cagle's joyful laughter boomed out as he scooped her up in his arms and swung her around. Suddenly he sobered and flushed as he noticed the encircling group of amused Indians. He put her down and cleared his throat. "I, uh . . .

I jest thought I'd drop by and see if the youngun needs anything," Cagle said. "I reckon you-all will be movin' south soon . . ." he added hesitantly, looking down at the girl.

Grazing Fawn smiled bleakly as her son translated. The trapper had come two days out of his way to "drop by"! They belong together, she thought, sad at the thought of losing the child. The Indian woman was glad she had prepared herself for it. She respected Cagle even more when he did not ask for the return of Yellow Leaf. He had even brought Grazing Fawn a bolt of fine red cloth to make dresses for herself and the girl. He was an honorable man. Because he had asked her to take the girl, Cagle considered the deal closed.

The Indian woman had seen many summers. She had a husband and sons, so she was wise about men and their proud ways. The trapper's pride would not allow him to go back on his word or plead for Yellow Leaf's return. She would have to force him to take the child.

Black Bear looked shocked for a moment, then dutifully translated his mother's words. "I'm sorry, but you will have to take the girl with you. I am old, and the winters make my bones ache, even in the south. I have taught her much and kept her well for you, so I have earned the prime beaver skins you left to pay for her keep. If I am still here next summer, and the next, I will tend her, but you must come for her each fall."

Cagle saw the pain in her eyes and his face softened. "Thank you," he murmured, clasping the fragile hand in his for a moment.

"Well, here I am, stuck with you again. Shoulda knowed better'n to drop by," Cagle complained as he rode off down the trail with Yellow Leaf seated in front of him. "You kin see, don't nobody want you — not even yer own people. What I shoulda done was to jump on my horse and ride on off while thet young buck was still a'talkin' his mama's words!" But his craggy face was split in a wide and joyful grin.

Happy and content, Yellow Leaf clutched her doll and leaned her sturdy back against him. She had almost forgotten the meaning of most of his words but the tone of his voice was easy to understand. He loved her, and she was going home.

During the next eight years Cagle and Yellow Leaf were apart during every summer, to the girl's sorrow. If Grazing Fawn was not at the river yet, she was left with another family. The trapper had gradually pieced together the story of the removal of her tribe and many others. He was disturbed by the unjustness of it when he saw other small roving bands of Indians who had been allowed to remain. Why Yellow Leaf's family? Why not all, or none?

"Our small tribe was not on the army's list when the soldiers came," one brave told him. "We hid in the mountains and said we were Blackfoot, because we had heard they were not to be removed," another said. "Your President Andrew Jackson is hated more than any other white man!" one young brave spat. "Indian warriors fought beside him and helped make him a national hero. Yet he had no feeling for us and betrayed us when he became the president. He insulted the very brave who killed to save his life in a battle, when he was sent to plead that our people be allowed to remain on the land guaranteed to us by treaty. He, like all frontiersmen and settlers, thought it unbearable that the best farming land in the country should belong to Indians. He defied the white Congress and others sympathetic to our cause. He drove us out to humiliation, misery, and death!"

Although the entire tragedy was too much for the

20

simple trapper to fully comprehend, Cagle felt ashamed of being white as he listened to the laments of an old brave who had lost his family. "I was left behind because I am sick and old. But who can buy or sell the earth? Can any man own the winds?" he asked.

"Who could answer such questions?" Cagle wondered. He continued to question Indians he met, but none of them knew Yellow Leaf or her family. Every winter he worried about his age and felt that he was being selfish. The girl belonged with her own people; loving her wouldn't make her white. Thus Cagle left her every spring, determined that each time would be the last time he would see her. But he missed her and was haunted by the sad dark eyes. He cursed himself for his weakness, but every autumn he found himself retracing his trail before the Indians broke up the river camp and moved south. He knew Grazing Fawn would not abandon her, and he always pretended that he would check on her, then leave, but he was never able to resist her plea, "Take me home, Cagle. Please take me with you. Just this one winter."

CHAPTER 3

As she grew older, Yellow Leaf periodically left him and moved into a bark tepee she had made on the shore of a nearby lake where they fished. The trapper never knew why. Maybe he had made her angry. Or perhaps she was practicing a religion he couldn't understand and merely needed to be alone. Cagle worried about her at first, but he knew she would return when she was ready, and not before. The cabin was lonely without her, but he soon grew accustomed to the absences. He was always happy and relieved when he awoke to find her moving about the fireplace as though she had never been away, preparing breakfast.

The cabin had now been expanded by a lean-to where Cagle slept. This left the warmer large room for Yellow Leaf. It was a long narrow room with the fireplace at one end, comfortably furnished with crude furniture Cagle had made. Very little light seeped through small windows covered with hides that he had scraped very thin and oiled. An apt pupil, Yellow Leaf had learned many things from the Indian women. She made clay bowls, baskets, and thick mats that added to their comfort. She could sew, clean the cabin, and cook tasty meals in an iron pot suspended from a metal hook wedged between stones in the fireplace. Their differing skills worked well together.

Since he was relieved of preparing meals and other household chores, Cagle was able to lay more traps and service them. No matter how late he returned, the cabin was warm, and food was ready. Then Yellow Leaf worked beside him skinning and stretching pelts. Having a woman —even a young girl—around made his life easier. For the first time Cagle, who had never considered himself a family man, wondered how different his life might have been if he had taken a wife and fathered a family. "But it's too late now," the trapper sighed. "I'm too old and set in my ways to change. Even if a woman could stand lookin' at this battered old face of mine, which ain't likely."

As the snows melted again, and the trees flushed red at the tips of their branches Yellow Leaf grew tense with dread. Soon Cagle would be loading his skins for the long trip to market them. He would go to a frontier town she had only heard about. And again she would be left with whatever band of strange Indians happened to be camped near the junction of the rivers 30 miles away—maybe forever! Cagle had returned for her before, but she couldn't be certain he would again. Who would clean her beautiful cabin, cook the trapper's food, and prepare herbs for the coughing spells that plagued him all winter? Cagle was growing older and tired easily. Couldn't he see how badly he needed her?

As she sat cross-legged on a fur rug where she was sewing in the light from the fireplace, Yellow Leaf broached the subject. She didn't look up from the porcupine quill and bead design she was sewing on the moccasins she had cut out for him. The trapper sat at the table, using a whetstone to hone already razor-sharp knives. "You won't be leaving me with the Indians again this spring, Cagle," she said softly. She didn't let it sound like a question.

"O'course I will, youngun!" the grizzled trapper retorted as he shifted a wad of chewing tobacco to the other jaw and tested a knife edge with his thumb. "And I ain't a'fetchin' you no more! Don't know why I did afore. Shoulda forgot about you thet first spring. I've tole you a hunnert times. You ain't no kin and no responsibility of mine! Besides, yer practically a full-growed woman now, bein' Injun. S'time you was choosin' some young buck fer a future husband instead of livin' out here with an old mossback that don't owe you nothin'!"

Yellow Leaf rose to her full height, which was only slightly higher than the trapper's waist, and stared at him with angry, smoldering eyes. Reminded suddenly of the little girl who had so violently objected to having her necklaces removed, Cagle stopped chewing and watched her warily. He halfway expected her to fly across the room and strike him.

"No, Cagle!" she cried. "I won't let you leave me behind again. If you do, I'll run away and follow you. You're my family. You're all I have. I'm going with you to sell the pelts, and then I'm coming home again!" Her face was set and determined.

"Ah, well. You've never been nothin' but a thorn in my flesh. Don't know what I ever done bad enough to deserve sech a burden, but it's fer sure that I'm saddled with you. Won't nobody else take you!" the aging trapper said bitterly.

He knew she meant it. "Women! There ain't no reasonin' with 'em, no matter what age or what color they be! Not even fer their own good," he snorted. He flung open the door and stalked out.

"He'll keep me! He won't go away without me again!" Yellow Leaf thought, almost limp with relief as she sagged down and started working again. All she wanted was to be with Cagle and take care of him. His brusqueness didn't fool her. Tragedy and chance had thrown them together, but the trapper loved her as much as she did him. She had learned long ago to disregard his words. It was the tone of his voice and the look in his eyes that really mattered.

From her vantage point atop the pile of roped-down pelts, Yellow Leaf's eyes glistened with excitement as she saw her first town. Cagle had told her about it many times, but it wasn't like seeing one firsthand. She caught her breath as she saw beautiful plumed ladies' hats in a milliner's store window, behind real glass! But they looked less lovely when she noticed the stuffed bluebird mounted on a pink velvet bonnet, its poor pinned wings spread wide. And how many trees were felled so the crowds of white people (more than she had ever seen in her life!) could walk with dry moccasins in rain or snow, she wondered, as she contemplated the wide wooden sidewalks lining each side of the main street that ran through the center of the town. It seemed a terrible waste when one considered the number of cabins that might have been built from so many logs.

Spots of color burned on her high cheekbones when she became aware of jeers and the crowd following them. She lowered her eyes to the dusty street and felt her heart begin to pound with fear. Cagle had warned her. "White folks get nervous and skittish when they see an Injun. Any Injun! No matter if it's broad daylight and smack in the center of town. And you cain't blame some of 'em too much. Not when so many whites has seen their whole family masacreed by bloodthirsty scalpin' redskins," he reminded. "So you jest hold yer tongue and don't provoke 'em none. We'll sell our skins, do some tradin', and then clear out jest as soon as we can."

He looked grim, but Cagle nodded and then ignored the unsmiling row of men seated on benches against the building where they stopped. None of them nodded back.

They just stood up and stared. The trapper pretended not to hear the shouts as he reached strong arms to help Yellow Leaf. Nothing on earth, except Cagle's determined face, could have persuaded the terrified girl to dismount in the jostling mob. She could almost smell their hatred! Loosening her tight grip on the rope reins, she took a deep holding breath, then obediently slid down into Cagle's arms.

"Squaw man! Living with Injuns! No wonder you stay out in the woods, Cagle. How many squaws you got yerself out there? And how many half-breed younguns?" a man taunted, his face horribly twisted with rage.

"Redskin! Heathen! No good Injun savage!" a youth her own size shouted and then spat full in her face. The cowering and bewildered Yellow Leaf could feel Cagle tremble with suppressed rage as she clung to him. He gently wiped her face with his hand, then protectively shoved her between him and the mule as he turned to face them. He hadn't expected this much commotion, although he had thought they would be greeted with some hostility.

A few people drifted away looking ashamed, but most of the frenzied hecklers remained, pushing and shoving. One particularly obnoxious man, taller and much younger than Cagle, stood toe to toe with him, hurling curses and obscenities into the trapper's ashen face. Cagle tried to shove the man aside, so they could pass through, but the people pushed closer, which narrowed the small circle. Yellow Leaf's stricken eyes looked for a gap, but they were trapped! They were like a wolf pack closing in for the kill. Suddenly someone tripped her and she went sprawling under the mule. She buried her face in her arms, afraid the skittish mule would trample her as the crowd swirled around them. She could hear some of the spectators making bets on the outcome of the brewing fight. They were shouting encouragement to the local man.

These were the first whites she had ever been around, and she was stunned at the howling mob. She had never seen Indians so savage and angry! Why did they have so much hatred for her? But her concern was for Cagle now, more than for herself. She winced at each thud of hard blows against flesh. It wasn't a fair fight. Youth was on the side of the younger man. The trembling girl raised her head as Cagle groaned and went down again. There was a sickening crack as his head hit the edge of the wood sidewalk. He limply sagged down into the dust, his head bent at a peculiar angle. "He's dead! Cagle's dead!" Yellow Leaf whispered in horrified disbelief.

"It was an accident. I didn't mean to kill him. I was just trying to teach him a lesson about bringin' redskins into town. It was just a fistfight . . . you all saw it," the other man protested to the suddenly hushed crowd. No one seemed to notice as the Indian girl darted between two buildings and raced away. Running like the wind, her sides aching, Yellow Leaf reached the safety of a grove of tall trees she had noticed as they entered the town. Sobbing, she flung herself down. "No! No, Cagle! No!" she cried over and over, pounding at the earth with her fists.

CHAPTER 4

The exhausted Yellow Leaf had slept and drawn strength from the cool rich soil. She marveled at the way nothing had changed with Cagle's death. The sun still shone, patches of fragile wild flowers were dotted throughout the trees like drifts of colored snow, and a light wind ruffled vivid new green oak leaves. Overhead a redbird perched on a swaying top branch and whistled to his mate. She answered him from the forest that seemed to cower away from the town.

The girl felt neither hunger nor thirst as she sat, knees bent, her chin resting on folded arms, thinking. Where could she go now? Back to the Indians? To the cabin that would be unbearably lonely without the trapper? Or was it time to head west to the Indian Territory and try to find her own tribe and family—if they had survived the march? How would they recognize each other? Except for short flashes of a memory of two small boys—her brothers?—and a beautiful dusky face that must have been her mother's, she could only remember the white trapper. The woman had worn a necklace exactly like Yellow Leaf's favorite. She thought she remembered how the swinging copper medallion caught the light as the woman bent over a cooking fire. "Do I really remember, or is it all just a dream?" Yellow Leaf sighed.

Grief overwhelmed her again as she remained hidden and watched a few men bury Cagle on a barren hill in a small cemetery north of the town. They stopped often to drink from a bottle they passed around. How could they laugh and joke while digging a man's grave? Hatred for whites — all whites, except Cagle — swept over her so powerfully that she trembled with it. "I'm Indian. Indian!" she whispered fiercely. "I won't forget again!"

"Hate is a waste," Cagle had said once. "Hurts the hater more'n the hated. Jest plain curdles the food in a man's stomach. Makes you weaker and yore enemies stronger. Like shootin' a bear with an empty gun. Why let another man make *yore* heart pound, or mebby throw you into a killin' fit? Never wasted no time on it myself. I like to enjoy my vittles."

As she considered the misery in the pit of her stomach, Yellow Leaf concluded that the trapper was right. But for the moment, at least, she couldn't seem to stop hating once she had started. White men had first robbed her of her parents, and now Cagle, the only one she had left to love. She winced and stiffened with new pain as one of the men plunged his shovel deep into the mound of raw earth and wiped his face with a shirt sleeve.

Even after the men had left, she couldn't withdraw her gaze from the mound of moist dirt. It looked so lonely; and ugly, like a scar in the earth. Had they buried Cagle properly? Would he rest here, she wondered, shivering with superstitious dread. Yellow Leaf had never seen a white man's burial before, but it seemed all wrong somehow. She preferred the more ceremonial Indian custom. There should have been sorrow and chants, the slow beat of a mourning drum. Cagle was a great and good man. He should not have had to sneak unnoticed from this world into the next.

Thinking of his unexpected death reminded her of their horse, the pelts, and the mule — all still inside the town. She had worked hard beside Cagle. With the trapper gone, they rightfully belonged to her, not the white murderers, for she thought all were equally guilty of his death. After dark she would reenter the town, find them, and steal them back if necessary.

She was surprised and disappointed when the town remained so busy long after sundown. Light spilled into the street through swinging doors, and patiently waiting horses lined the hitching racks in front of them. Yellow Leaf heard drunken shouts and raucous laughter as she slipped among the shadows. Then the sound of a piano, hymns, and handclapping drew her past the place where the fight had taken place. Posts had been driven into the ground and a roof made of saplings and fresh tree branches. Lanterns swung from cross poles, casting flickering light over a crowd. It was a preaching service.

Unable to resist the music, Yellow Leaf crept closer and crouched down between two wagons to listen. The rousing songs seemed to quicken their spirits and make the people happy. They even made her feel better. A chubby toddler with yellow curls sat on his mother's lap, rocking and clapping his dimpled hands. The Indian girl smiled as she watched him.

Everything changed when the music stopped again and a fat little man began to bounce around the raised platform, his powerful voice rising and lowering almost hypnotically as he attacked the suddenly hushed crowd. Yellow Leaf was mystified by his fit of rage and wondered why the people would tolerate the abuse he heaped upon them. She was awed and shaken as the bald and perspiring man rose on his toes, raised clenched fists to the sky, and shrieked out the horrors and torture of hell—the destination of all his listeners, according to the traveling preacher, who could hardly have known them.

31

Both the Indian girl and the audience jumped with fright as he suddenly slapped his hands together, like a clap of doom. "Yes, sinners," he thundered, "that's exactly where you're headed. You and you and you," he added, pointing his pudgy finger like a rifle as he turned. "Right straight into Satan's fiery furnace! And once you're in the midst of those searing flames, lost in clouds of sulfur and brimstone, a'cryin' and a'beggin' for mercy, you're going to remember this night, friends."

The hushed audience leaned forward as his voice dropped to a whisper. "You'll remember this night because there ain't going to be any mercy! You'll be without hope; your immortal souls lost for eternity. Yes, brothers and sisters, you're going to be worse off than any heathen Indian — who ever'body knows ain't got no soul a'tall. None to save and none to lose. No more than dogs, cats and horses . . ."

Shocked, Yellow Leaf pondered the statement. Cagle had said people were all the same once you got past their hides. Just good or bad. The trapper couldn't read or write, but he had heard a lot of preaching, he had said. At times he had talked to her about heaven and hell. She had assumed he meant that she, too, would end up in one or the other place when she died. But Cagle could have been wrong. Or maybe he had temporarily forgotten she wasn't white. Cagle knew all about trapping, and a real preacher ought to know all about his business too. Since the man had said it, she could no longer count on being included.

Actually, being banished from hell was a big relief to her after the preacher's vivid and terrifying description of it. And since she had barely escaped, she suddenly felt sorry for all those poor white sinners. Some of them were pallid with fear and already fanning themselves!

32

During the long winters, when they had talked about many things, Cagle admitted that men who read the Holy Book and professed to believe in it did not always practice its teachings. If she didn't have a soul, Yellow Leaf was certain she had a spirit, which satisfied her. She believed in the spirit world and a future life similar to the one on earth, only better. There would be no cold, hunger, or thirst because there would be enough of everything for everyone. When an Indian reached this destination, he would be greeted with a feast prepared in his honor, and there would be songs and dances of joy. Considering the brutality of white people and their broken promises, she lost all faith in the preacher. Yellow Leaf felt only scorn for the fat little man who would send the beautiful baby boy to hell.

Yellow Leaf left the preaching behind and worked her way toward the livery stable. Cagle had loved to talk, and she had listened well, eager to know about a world she had never seen. She was familiar with the town and the customs of its citizens, to some extent. Travelers rented a room at the hotel, which was the tallest building in town, and they boarded their horses in the big barn at one end of the street. The horse and mule were probably there.

After she had listened outside the double doors, the Indian girl slipped inside and checked the stalls until she found Cagle's horse. The mule was in the next compartment. "The pelts! Where are they?" she whispered, almost sick with disappointment. Her sudden appearance had startled the horse. Engrossed in calming him, she didn't notice the big man who suddenly grabbed her from behind. Her frantic efforts to free herself were useless as he half dragged and half carried her toward the door, yelling for the sheriff.

"It's Cagle's breed youngun, Sheriff. I figured she'd

come sneakin' back to steal the horses, so I been laying for her!" the man shouted as a small crowd gathered.

Prepared for the worst and hoping to meet her fate bravely, Yellow Leaf stood quietly, her eyes staring through them. She expected no mercy. They had, after all, destroyed Cagle, who was white and one of them. "What do you mean 'steal,' Hiller? Being Cagle's girl, she's got a right to think they belong to her, now that he's dead, doesn't she?" the man wearing a badge said. He made no effort to mask his dislike for the stable owner. He was struck by the dignity and beauty of the girl. Cagle's white blood doesn't show on her, he thought. The large black eyes, rosy copper skin, and thick braids that reached almost to her waist must have come straight from her mother. There was nothing of a white father about her.

"Do you understand English?" he asked Yellow Leaf gently. Surprised at the tone of his voice, the girl glanced briefly at him, then stared straight ahead again. She had decided to remain silent. She would learn more if they thought she couldn't understand. But she felt safer now, because of the lawman.

There was a lot of bickering back and forth about what to do with her later, in the jail, where the pelts were piled in a corner. Her heart was heavy as she remembered Cagle's hard work all winter. "Never had me a better trappin' season," he had boasted proudly when they were loading the mule.

Yellow Leaf sat impassively, hardly listening. She glanced longingly at the bunk inside the bars that split the large room in half. She was so tired now that she didn't care what the white men decided.

"I don't want my family in the same town with no stinkin' Injun! It ain't safe, Sheriff. You got to do something," one man kept insisting. "We'd be well shed of her if you'd give her the mounts and the pelts and shoo her out of town. She'd find her way back to her maw. When her and Cagle don't show up, there's liable to be a whole bunch of 'em pour into town. And once they find out what happened to him, there's no telling what they might do!"

"We can't do that, Simpson," the sheriff disagreed. "Those skins are valuable property. And for all we know, Cagle's got a white wife and family somewhere too. Legally they'd be the ones entitled to these furs, not his Indian family. We'll just have to wait till the judge comes around and decides what's legal and proper. Right now we've got to find a place for her to stay. She's big enough to earn her keep. Any of you needing some help for your wives?"

"My woman's ailing — expecting another baby any day now," one man ventured. "She could use some help with the work and the other little 'uns until she gets her strength back. But I don't know about no Injun . . . " he added doubtfully.

"We're not talking about a buck warrior with a tomahawk!" the sheriff said disgustedly. "This here is just a slip of a girl. And being Cagle's kid, she's got to be partly civilized. She'll probably be a big help if your wife will make signs to tell her what to do. Take her on home with you," the lawman said, settling the matter.

She could see the man was sorry he had mentioned it. Mounted on a horse behind him, she dozed in spite of her fear. The man hadn't said a word to her, just motioned her to sit behind him. He plainly didn't like her, but she would work hard, and perhaps the white woman would be kind. Cagle had no white family to be found, so the judge would surely give her the pelts when he came. No one had to know the trapper wasn't her father. Cagle hadn't denied it.

When they reached the sagging log house a few miles outside of town, the man dismounted and motioned her to remain on the horse. Once the door had closed, Yellow Leaf slid off and slipped to a window. The man was explaining about her to a tired looking blond woman. Behind them, the girl could see three small children sleeping in one bed.

"An Indian in this house? Never!" the woman cried. "I wouldn't sleep a wink. What about my grandmother's brooch and my gold ring? You know how savages love jewelry. She'd steal us blind — or worse! We could all be scalped and murdered in our beds! Big or little, they're all the same. Just naturally cruel and bloodthirsty! Everybody knows they can't be civilized. What kind of man are you? Why didn't you refuse to bring her here? I won't have her near me or my children!"

The man was still trying to reason with his hysterical wife as Yellow Leaf turned away, went back to the horse, and walked him back toward the road. When she was well away from the house, she mounted and galloped back toward town, hoping it was the only horse the family owned. She would be more careful this time, but she was determined to get Cagle's horse and go home. The townspeople would be asleep by now, and they thought they were rid of her. If she left the farmer's horse and forgot about the pelts, she sensed that even the sheriff would be relieved to have her gone.

At the edge of town, Yellow Leaf tied the lathered horse to a small tree and slipped around the stable. No one was on the street and the buildings were all dark. A lantern over the stable entrance had been turned low. She eased through the door and stopped. Listening, with every sense alert, she followed snores to a pile of straw. The man who had grabbed her was sprawled out asleep, an empty bottle beside him. She wrinkled her nose at the foul smell.

Yellow Leaf didn't turn her back this time. She kept wary eyes fastened on him as she uncoiled a new rope from the rafters and cautiously crept toward him. She pounced like a hungry puma, winding the rope around him as he thrashed awake. When he opened his mouth to shout, she shoved in a handful of straw, then gagged him with his neckerchief. The man's eyes bulged with terror as she tightened the knot, then secured the rope binding his arms. With another halter rope, she bound his ankles. She rose and stared down at him. She was shaken by her emotions. It was the first time she had ever wanted to strike and beat another human. She stepped back and covered him loosely with straw. He was trussed up tightly enough to stay there until a customer found him the next morning. She wouldn't have to worry about his sounding an alarm about her escape.

"I wanted to hurt you, but I didn't. You're lucky. For a few seconds I saw you as representing all white men, which your town has taught me to hate. I'm *not* a heathen savage! And I wouldn't know how to scalp anybody if I wanted to!" she spat at the heaving mound of yellow straw.

She was an expert bareback rider, so all Yellow Leaf needed was a blanket and rope reins, which Cagle's horse was used to. She stroked the mule's velvety nose. How she wished she could take him back home too, but she would have to travel too fast. She led the horse out and around the barn, then on behind the buildings along the main street.

She stayed off the road until she passed the grove of trees where she had hidden all day. Had she and Cagle only ridden into the town this morning? So much had happened, it seemed a week ago. She stopped once and glanced off toward the grave she couldn't see in the dark.

"I've learned all I ever want to know about white people, Cagle," she whispered as she mounted and rode toward home. The trip would take several days, but no one would see her. She would travel at night and sleep during the day.

CHAPTER 5

When she had traveled three nights with no sign of pursuit, Yellow Leaf began to feel safe. She had spent most of the time trying to decide about her future. The trip west would be very difficult at best. And since she had no real destination and no assurance that her family was alive or that she could find them if they were, she had regretfully decided to wait until the following spring to start the long journey. She thought about the lost furs with bitterness. The money they represented would have made all the difference.

Decisively she headed east, out of her way, to the Indian camp. She would not stay with them, but she needed seeds. They would help her. She would have to work hard to prepare for a winter alone in the cabin, but Cagle had been a good teacher. She felt confident that she could do it. There was time to plant pumpkin, squash, beans, and corn, to harvest in late summer. She would preserve fish and meat. By setting a small line of Cagle's traps in the fall, she would have fresh meat and some pelts to trade or sell when spring came.

The trail down to the river camp was a homecoming of sorts. The horse knew his way, so Yellow Leaf released her hold on the reins. She had played along here with groups of Indian children each summer for as long as she could remember. Each tree and boulder was familiar. She could have made every twist and turn in total darkness, without bumping into anything or missing a turn. It was strange that she had never missed this place or her friends, once she left it with Cagle. Not even during the long winters. Throughout her life it was thoughts of the cabin and Cagle that brought an aching homesick feeling back to her, never the Indian village.

Halfway down the long hill Yellow Leaf stopped and surveyed the sprawling camp, searching for familiar tepees. Some were made of hides and painted with symbols; others were frames, covered with bark. Each family group was set up slightly apart from the others. The camp was actually composed of many separate units.

She was overjoyed when her keen eyes lit on Grazing Fawn's tepee. Quickly she urged the horse toward it. The warmth and concern on the woman's face, weathered and wrinkled like brown tree bark, brought tears to Yellow Leaf's eyes as they clasped hands. She hadn't expected to find her still alive this spring. "And this will be her last," the girl thought sadly as she saw how feeble the woman was. She warmed the thin cold hands in her own strong ones for a moment, then led Grazing Fawn back to the buffalo robe in front of the cone-shaped home she remembered so well.

"You are alone now, and you have the trapper's horse. He has died during the winter?" Grazing Fawn asked as she knelt and wearily resumed grinding corn between two flat stones. There were only a few handfuls of light yellow meal in the clay pot beside her, and it was too coarse. "Why do people have to get old and helpless?" the girl mourned. She remembered how Grazing Fawn used to make her grind the meal again and again until it was just right. She had demanded perfection in weaving and in everything else she taught her. Now she was too old and sick to care.

Gently Yellow Leaf took the smaller stone from her

and began to grind with swift sure strokes. "Cagle is four days dead, but he did not die during the winter. He was slain by his own people when we entered the white man's town to sell the pelts. Oh, Grazing Fawn, he's dead because of me. It's my fault! He would have been safe alone."

"Aiii," the old woman sighed, as she watched the girl's tears bead and roll in the flour dust. The clay pot filled rapidly as Yellow Leaf talked and worked out her sorrow and frustration. Grazing Fawn would have fine meal for too many days unless she stopped soon. "And those same white men call *us* heathens and savages!" the old woman croaked with bitterness when Yellow Leaf stopped talking and sank back to rest.

As she looked at the beautiful face of the one she called Summer Daughter, streaked with flour and tears shed for the death of a white man, Grazing Fawn wondered again how her people had been so easily defeated. How weak the whites must be, to be so full of hate and terror at the mere sight of this child of double sorrow in their town. If only the red man had known how dishonest and brutal the invaders were and had driven them back! The first who came must have been good men, like Cagle, she decided. And because of that, the Indians had befriended and helped the evil, land-hungry ones as well, not seeing the danger until they had spread across the land like a plague. "I've lived too long—too long," she sighed bleakly.

Grazing Fawn did not try to dissuade Yellow Leaf from wintering alone, nor from making her trip the following spring. It was a useless quest, she thought privately, but even an impossible goal was better than none. It provided a reason for fighting . . . and living. She herself had no goal, no quest. The years were a heavy burden, and she was weary of life now that her sons were braves and her husband dead.

While Yellow Leaf rested, Grazing Fawn went among the tepees, gathering seeds and herbs the women had brought from different areas. She laid them near the sleeping girl. Love softened the clouded and dim eyes as she watched her even breathing. "Mother Earth and Father Sky," she prayed, "be kind to this lonely and unnamed child. Lead her to her own tribe and her parents." She removed a silver and turquoise bracelet from her arm. It was the only thing she owned of value. She did not know how old it was but it had been her mother's and her mother's mother's before that. The turquoise was a holy stone; it would help protect the girl. She laid it beside the bundle of seeds, then she went away. Both of them knew this farewell would be the last. It was better to avoid it.

A spasm of pain and loneliness crossed Yellow Leaf's face as the weary horse plodded toward the cabin in the clearing. How beautiful it looked in the red and purple sunset! If only the trapper was waiting inside, sitting at the table honing his knives. But he wasn't. And he never would be again. Grateful for the food Grazing Fawn had given her, the tired girl tended the horse before going inside to eat.

She built a small twig fire to take away the dampness and sat gazing into the dancing flames that were lashed and tipped with blue. Perhaps she should have stayed at the village with Grazing Fawn. Grieving, Yellow Leaf thought about Cagle and wished his spirit well. It was lonely here, and it would be worse when the snows came. But the cabin was snug. It was home and where she wanted most to be. "Maybe I don't belong in either world, the red man's or the white man's. Suppose I never find my family and peace. I'll never know who I am!" she whispered. She scattered the embers, then went to her bunk and fell asleep almost before she had straightened out.

Food and firewood would be her most pressing need. During the next few days Yellow Leaf was too busy to dwell on Cagle's absence. Since she had no plow, the Indian girl dug circles of loosened soil and planted the precious seeds in their centers. Her small body was wiry, but she was not strong enough to swing the heavy axe as tirelessly as the trapper, so she used the horse to drag in fallen trees. The dead wood was brittle enough to easily chop into lengths to fit the fireplace. Saving every twig, she felt elated as the stacks of logs and branches outside the cabin grew larger every day. A stack higher than her head was beside the cabin door, for use in severe weather when blizzards or deep snows might prevent her reaching the larger piles. She placed it on the north side where it would block out part of the cold winds that would batter and leak in around the heavy wood door.

When the garden needed no tending, and her muscles were sore from swinging the axe, Yellow Leaf went to the lake for fish and turtles, which were plentiful. The Indians had taught her how to prepare and preserve food. She used hickory wood to cure the meat slowly over hot embers. When it was smoked, she chopped strong vines to tie it in the rafters of the cabin, to protect the food from animals and insects. In late summer she dug pits and buried turnips and other produce between layers of dried weeds so they would not rot. The vegetables and wild fruit would not freeze, and she could dig out as much as she needed, then cover them again. She gathered more herbs for medicine to treat illnesses she might have during the winter.

Daily she remembered to thank the Great Spirit for the earth, which was not only beautiful but supplied every need if one took only as much as was needed — which the greedy white men did not understand, according to the Indians. As she had often slipped away to enlist the help

43

of the Great Spirit when Cagle had been ill or his traps netted few pelts, which always helped, she now left baskets of fish and food in the forest and near the lake, to show her appreciation.

CHAPTER 6

The summer raced' away almost before she noticed. With the first heavy frosts Yellow Leaf competed with the gray squirrels for nuts that fell. She burst into laughter as one darted up a tree and chattered his outrage at her intrusion. "There are enough for both of us," she chided. But he twitched his tail and skittered into a hole in the hollow tree and watched begrudgingly as she filled her basket.

Yellow Leaf's physical needs were taken care of. She had a snug home, food, and fuel enough to last the winter. She freed the horse to forage for himself, hoping to find him again in the spring. But her craving for companionship could not be satisfied. It was a constant hunger that food and drink could not lull. For too many generations her people had been accustomed to living in groups. With Cagle gone, her spirit instinctively yearned for a tribe of her own people.

Two days after the first blizzard Yellow Leaf returned from running the line of traps near the lake. She was clumsy and bearlike in her bed furs, which she wore to fend off the bitter cold. Kneeling, she groaned with fatigue as she shrugged off the bundle of frozen game bound to her back and turned to stir up the fire. The snares had been difficult to locate under the fresh snow, and her catch had been small. Only two rabbits and a young wolf.

Later as Yellow Leaf squatted near the fire, cooking bits of meat over the flames, she was startled by a whimper from the pile of game she had put near the heat to thaw before attempting to dress the meat.

She prodded the pile with a stick and leaped back as the wolf stirred feebly and stared up at her, baring his fangs, and growls rumbling deep in his throat. The Indian girl crouched, then raised the stick and crept closer, to aim a crushing blow at the animal's head.

As she stood over the helpless wolf, Yellow Leaf was suddenly shaken by the brave hopelessness in the stricken animal's eyes. For a few seconds the two stared into each other's faces — a gaze that sparked a momentary bond of kinship in the girl. Cagle had never allowed her to have a pet. Animals were food and pelts, nothing more. Yellow Leaf was confused by the rush of sympathy she felt. The wolf's coat was prime. It would have been her first good pelt.

On impulse Yellow Leaf turned and picked up the dropped roasting stick with the half-raw meat skewered on the end of it. She offered the meat gingerly. As the starved wolf tried to draw back, his growls rose hysterically, then changed to pitiful whimpers as the useless hind legs refused to budge. The trap had injured his back.

Again the girl offered the food. The wild one slavered in a frenzy of hunger, but he would not eat. Yellow Leaf removed the meat from the stick and tossed it near the wolf.

The Indian girl toasted more meat over the fire and ate it, watching the animal as it stretched its nose closer to the food. Whining, he sniffed it suspiciously, turning yellowish, tawny eyes to stare at the girl, who watched without moving. The animal had seen few humans, and every instinct warned of danger. Sadly Yellow Leaf watched as the wolf twisted and turned, straining to straighten his legs. Again she felt the sudden rush of pity and understanding as he turned yearning eyes away from the door. He laid the long muzzle on his forepaws and bravely prepared to die.

When Yellow Leaf awoke at dawn, she was surprised to find the animal still living. The wolf growled threateningly as the mound of hides stirred, then bared his fangs viciously as she sat up. Yellow Leaf quickly reached for the heavy stick, then laid it aside when she saw that the wolf was still helpless and had not moved.

Suddenly she laughed. The wolf had lapped the water from a pot she had shoved near him, and the chunk of meat had vanished. Somehow, though they were enemies, it gave her a warm feeling to have a living creature to share her home and food. It eased the bitter burden of loneliness to feel the wary eyes watching as she moved about the cabin. "I shall call you Naantam, which means wolf," she said.

Returning from the trap line, Yellow Leaf's snowshoes felt lighter because Naantam waited. His injured back was healing slowly, and he could limp around the cabin now. But she was still frightened of him, even though she knew she would never be able to kill him. So one day Yellow Leaf offered Naantam his freedom by leaving the door open. Tears began to slip down her cheeks as he quickly rose and crossed the cabin to leave her. For long moments the wolf stood in the doorway, ears perked, hungrily sniffing the frigid air. His body trembled with eagerness. Then his ears twitched at the sound of a low hiccoughing sob, and the tawny yellow eyes looked back at her. More tears, but of happiness now, slipped down her face when he unexpectedly returned and curled up in front of the fireplace. He couldn't leave her! Perhaps she should have named him Cagle! Did Naantam feel affection for her, or did he merely sense that he was still too weak to survive in such bitter weather? One icy morning she awoke to find Naantam curled on the bed fur at the bottom of her bunk. Now she was no longer afraid of him.

Day after day Yellow Leaf tended her traps with Naantam limping along beside her. The wolf made no attempt to hunt or escape. He seemed content with the rabbits and other small game the girl shared with him. Her pile of pelts seemed disappointingly small, compared to Cagle's, despite all her hard work. But the cold was gradually tapering off. It would soon be spring. Naantam seemed to sense it too. He had begun to leave her now, and sometimes she did not see him for several days. It was lonely without him, but he would have to return to the forest for good when she began her trip west. She hoped he would not have too much to learn again. Cagle had been wise not to let her tame wild things, she decided. It handicapped them, and how could they tell which humans to trust and which to avoid? This had been her own problem too, she thought.

When Naantam stayed gone two weeks, Yellow Leaf decided he wouldn't return again. She prayed that he hadn't been killed, but perhaps he had found a mate or joined a pack, which was as it should be. The frozen lake had water showing now, far out from the bank. The dawn and evening skies were often patched with bright blue against the blustery gray. Winter was dying. She would be preparing to leave soon.

Lost in her thoughts, for she felt torn about leaving, the girl carelessly stepped out of the trees and into the clearing. Fright clutched at her throat when she saw five Indian men. Their leader had dismounted from Cagle's horse! They were between her and the cabin. It was impossible to run in the clumsy snowshoes. She was trapped!

Rudely the men demanded food. Yellow Leaf nodded,

trying to conceal her fear. Although she was afraid of them, shame washed over her as she looked at the ragged little band of renegades. White men had reduced brave warriors to this!

The men had been changed by circumstances beyond their control and had little or no pride left. If Yellow Leaf had found them sitting quietly, waiting, she would have hastened to prepare food for them. But they would only have eaten after she insisted. They would never have shown they were suffering from cold or hunger. From such lack of good manners, she knew she was in danger.

"Where is your man?" the arrogant leader demanded, pointing to the two sets of snowshoe tracks in the snow.

Hope and relief flooded over the frightened girl. She had used Cagle's larger snowshoes for two days, before repairing her own. The men had noticed the different sizes and thought a husband or father was also living here.

She pointed back toward the lake. "He is tending his traps and will return soon," she replied steadily, her heart pounding, but hoping the lie would make them go away.

Sudden menacing growls behind her, and the superstitious fear on the faces of the Indians, made her feel braver. After being gone so long, Naantam had appeared from nowhere. He was crouched on the snowy slope slightly behind her, fangs bared and eyes gleaming! He was obviously protecting the girl.

The men grouped closer together, then fell back in confusion as she walked to the huge wolf, put her hand on the raised ridge of fur down his back, and talked soothingly to him.

"I will hold him while you leave," Yellow Leaf told them calmly. "And that is my man's horse you have found. Thank you for returning it."

For a heartstopping moment Yellow Leaf was afraid

she had gone too far in demanding the return of Cagle's horse. The leader stiffened and anger flashed in his black eyes. He looked from her to the wolf, standing quietly now but with watchful, restless eyes scanning the group.

Deliberately Yellow Leaf withdrew her hand from Naantam's back. The wolf immediately crouched again, powerful muscles ready to attack. The massive upper jaw wrinkled as he showed his teeth. "He will spring if you make any move toward us," she warned, as the leader seemed to signal one of his men, whose fingers inched toward a knife at his belt. The creeping fingers hesitated, then stopped.

Spots of angry red burned on the leader's cheeks, and he still held firmly to the rope around the horse's neck. It was an impasse. Yellow Leaf realized she had deeply humiliated him. She would have to offer him an honorable way out of the deadlock.

"I am sorry I cannot prepare food for you," Yellow Leaf apologized. "I am ashamed of his bad manners, but you can see that Naantam does not like strangers. I don't dare remove my hand to cook. But I have just taken three fat rabbits. I would be happy if you will accept them as a gift for returning our horse. I can throw them to one of your braves, then hold the wolf until you have gone."

The leader considered her offer, then nodded and dropped the rope. When the girl again placed her hand on the wolf's head, relaxing him, he turned and vanished into the trees. He walked with new dignity, a brave again. He did not look back as the nearest Indian caught the bundle of rabbits Yellow Leaf threw. He and the remaining men faded silently into the forest.

Trembling, and stiff from her tense stance in the cold, Yellow Leaf sagged down in the snow. She placed her arms around Naantam's neck and buried her face in the silvery tipped brown fur. The men would not return. Like most Indians, they believed that animals could be inhabited by the spirits of both friend and enemies.

Naantam had returned for what proved to be his last visit, and he had repaid the Indian girl for sparing his life.

CHAPTER 7

The signs of spring were quickening everywhere now. Sassafras trees had new leaves, still tightly wrapped, and Yellow Leaf ate her first spring salad made of wild lettuce and tender spears of poke. There were high winds and severe spring storms that made the earth tremble with thunder. Yellow Leaf began to feel a sense of urgency when she watched the flocks of migrating ducks and geese flying over. She envied the birds, who followed invisible trails with unerring instinct. Their long-dead ancestors still led them to their destinations farther south, and even told them when to go and when to return again. The geese were like strings of beads strewn across the skies. They all looked alike, so how did the birds know which vee formation to join? Stragglers fought to keep up, but they never seemed to get mixed up if another flight crossed their path. She had no such instinct to guide her to her family.

During the next few weeks Yellow Leaf worked almost as hard to prepare for her trip as she had in getting ready for the long winter alone. She hadn't planned to linger here. She had meant to just tie her furs on the horse and go away. Instead, the cabin began to mean even more to her now that she was about to leave it. Forever, she thought. She was sobered by the thought that she was entering a new and critical phase of her life. According to Cagle's guess, she was about 12 or 13 years old now. Old enough to leave her childhood behind.

But the cabin represented security. It would be a sanctuary to return to — or even dream about — if her mission failed. And she found that she could not bear to merely spring Cagle's good traps and leave them to rust away. Instead, she brought them in, as she and Cagle had always done. She greased the iron and stored them away with the ones she had not used. This greasing of the traps had always been a sad spring ritual for her. It meant that Cagle was going away, and she would be returning to the Indian camp. It was even more poignant this final spring.

The more Yellow Leaf thought about the cabin, the more troubled she felt. Other removed Indians had grown so homesick that they had escaped and returned to eastern homes. Perhaps her family, too, would be eager to return here with her. She felt more at peace once she decided to prepare the cabin for an eventual return. She packed away the mats, clay pots, and baskets she had made, along with Cagle's clothing and other personal things. She cleaned the cabin thoroughly, using sand to scour the rough plank floor until it looked new. When she was finished, everything was as she had always left it, for her return the following fall. But many falls might pass before she returned this time — if she ever did.

Then she began to worry because there was no lock. No one had ever taken it over before, but now someone might hear that Cagle was dead. He had filed papers on 100 acres here, after Grazing Fawn had told him he must come for her each fall. The papers meant that he owned it legally, and no one could take it away. He had said her name too was on them, but Indians seldom had any rights under the white man's law. How could she prevent someone's finding the deserted cabin and moving in? If her family returned here with her and the house was occupied, she had little hope of being able to force them out.

After mulling over the problem for several days, Yellow Leaf thought of a possible solution. "A picture drawing! I can draw one on the door. It might work and frighten squatters away."

No Indians would move into a place where someone had died. They feared lurking evil spirits. Often, when they fell ill, the medicine man said the sickness had come because they had unknowingly walked on the grave of an enemy. They would not recover until he had cleansed and treated them. In some tribes they had no further use for the wigwam if death visited their family, so they buried their dead relative inside it. Then they moved away and built a new home.

Yellow Leaf took the bright paints she had mixed to decorate clay bowls and sketched out her picture warning on the heavy cabin door. She drew a family of four, a symbol that meant smallpox, then three of the figures going away in death. Indians feared that disease more than any other, with good reason. In 1763, when the British were fighting Chief Pontiac, a general had ordered blankets from smallpox victims given as gifts to tribes free of the disease, to drastically reduce their numbers. The plan had worked so well that other white men had done the same. When smallpox struck, it could quickly wipe out an entire village.

Any roving trapper would know the meaning of the symbols and prefer to avoid such a contaminated place. Yellow Leaf thought it unlikely that a white family would find the remote cabin, but if so, the Indian drawing would discourage them, even though they couldn't read it. Most white women would refuse to occupy a squaw's vacant home. Their men would feel reluctant too, assuming the Indians might return at any time.

Pleased that she had thought of it, the girl decided her drawing was probably better than a lock, which could easily be broken off with a heavy stone.

Now that everything was finished here, she would leave at dawn. But she tossed restlessly, not sleeping well. The excitement about leaving was mixed with fear of what the future might bring. And there was a feeling of guilt, almost as though she were deserting Cagle.

Streaks of red light showed in the east as Yellow Leaf packed the horse. It looked like twilight instead of morning. At the edge of the forest, Yellow Leaf could not resist stopping her horse to look at the weathered cabin, although she had resolved to ride away without looking back. Cagle's cabin looked silvery gray in the morning mist; serene and comfortable. Would she ever see it again? she wondered. And would Naantam return here in the winter, hurt or searching for her? "Oh, Cagle," she murmured softly as she took a last lingering look at the home they had shared. "I would never have found the strength to leave if you had lived and needed me."

CHAPTER 8

The trip to the Indian camp was difficult because of the muddy trail and steep hills. Near sundown, when Yellow Leaf reached the river, she was surprised at the small number of tepees she saw. She should have expected it and waited a little longer. This was the earliest she had ever arrived, and the weather was unseasonably cold. All the spring storms and heavy rains had swollen creeks and flooded lowlands. Many of the migrating Indians were waiting for flooding to subside and for warmer weather to arrive.

The chilled and exhausted girl was greeted warmly as she led her horse through the campsite, searching for a familiar face. There was no wigwam in Grazing Fawn's favorite spot. Silently Yellow Leaf stood there a moment, looking at a few bits of charcoal that marked the woman's old cooking fire. She touched the silver and turquoise bracelet and her eyes blurred as she remembered the face of her summer mother. Early or late, she knew Grazing Fawn would not come again. "Why am I always left alone? Will I be robbed of everyone who knows or loves me?" she mourned. She turned quickly and left the lonely spot.

Yellow Leaf was invited into other tepees, but she smiled and shook her head. There had been so few familiar things in her short life; she would keep searching. Someone who knew her should be told that she had finally started the journey to find her parents. There was no other way to leave a message in the event that her parents were also still searching for her, had escaped, and might turn up in this area. It was a remote possibility after all these years, but Fate took many strange twists and turns, as Cagle had said often.

How happy she was when she saw Laughing Eyes, the wife of Bear Toes, carrying water from the river. The slim Indian woman, only a few years older than Yellow Leaf, had her first child now. A tiny daughter named Dancing Squirrel. Cagle had left her with the girl's parents one spring, when Grazing Fawn's family had arrived late. And they had worked and played together throughout their childhood. The girl-wife welcomed Yellow Leaf as a sister. "I didn't expect to see you again, now that Grazing Fawn is dead," she said. "Aiii, I'm sorry. I thought you had heard," she added softly, as the other girl caught her breath and bit her lip to keep from crying out. Now she could no longer tell herself that Grazing Fawn was still alive somewhere in the south, and just too feeble to make the trip to the river camp this spring. Yellow Leaf wished Laughing Eyes hadn't told her.

Bear Toes had gone away hunting as soon as they arrived here, so Laughing Eyes had been busy selecting a site and building a bark wigwam, which was almost finished. Yellow Leaf thought of Cagle again as she helped Laughing Eyes finish her home.

She had never been able to fully explain many Indian customs to him. The fact that the husband had nothing to do with the choice of a location, nor the building of his home, baffled him. "I didn't know a squaw was allowed to decide *anything*—even though I reckoned they'd have to do all the hardest work!" he had sniffed disapprovingly. "I've allers heard thar ain't nothin' lazier than a buck

Injun. Don't turn a hand 'cept fer the enjoyments of life—like dancin', huntin', and their wars."

Laughing Eyes giggled when Yellow Leaf told her about it. "A brave knows many things, but I would not allow Bear Toes to select the place or build my tepee!" she said emphatically. "I might have a sloping or easily flooded floor, and besides, we would go without food while he was doing woman's work of cutting bark and stuffing cracks with moss. Men are supposed to provide food for their families; women build tepees. I feel sorry for white women if they cannot rule their own homes. It seems very strange."

When Bear Toes returned, he did not mention the finished tepee. Like most braves, he would consider it beneath him to complain, approve, or even notice.

Yellow Leaf and Laughing Eyes sat watching respectfully as her husband ate in silence. When he had finished and lit his pipe for a quiet smoke, they satisfied their hunger. He was cold and wet and had traveled far to bring meat. Yellow Leaf did not take offense, although she and Cagle had always eaten together. She knew that if there had not been enough food for all of them, Bear Toes would have insisted that she and his wife eat first. His pride would not have allowed him to show his own hunger and fatigue. Such trials strengthen the spirit. But Cagle would not have understood this custom either. He had heard from other white men that braves mistreat their wives and force them to eat after they, the children, and even the family dogs had eaten. It was not true, but so many of their customs had been misunderstood and misinterpreted by the whites. Many false impressions had spread and taken root. It was impossible to change the white people's wrong beliefs.

Bear Toes was deeply concerned about Yellow Leaf's proposed trip. He urged her to forget about it. "The removed tribes have been scattered," he told her, "and there is much trouble in the West. You don't know the names or even the faces of your family. You may walk past them in some village without recognizing each other. If they are alive . . . and so many died . . . so many," he added, almost to himself.

"Settlers are crowding into the area, which was supposed to be set aside for Indians 'so long as the grass is green and the skies are blue,' and the dishonest white statesmen are encouraging this," Bear Toes added bitterly. "Hostile Indians, with their land threatened, kill them. They, in turn, are massacred by soldiers, who stalk them like wolves and kill even the women and babies. Red men are resentful of the new Indians driven onto their land. If you are caught by the soldiers, you will be confined for life on a desolate reservation where many die every year from lung fever or starvation. I have talked to a brave who lost his family and returned here. You would have no friends on either side. It would be a difficult and dangerous trip. I doubt that you would survive."

Yellow Leaf had considered many perils, but her fears had concerned the threat of accident or the elements. She had not realized there would be such danger from her own race, although she would instinctively avoid any contact with whites. Her voice trembled with fright. "I respect your warning, Bear Toes, and I thank you for your concern. But I-I must go, even if I die," she whispered bleakly. "A restless spirit pushes me to go. To search. I don't have the strength to resist."

His face impassive, Bear Toes nodded. He understood that she could not fight such a force. Not, at least, without the help of a strong medicine man, and there was none here to help her. He felt certain she would die, but there was nothing more he could do.

The young brave's face grew taut and angry when Yellow Leaf told about Cagle's senseless death and her experience in the white town. "I'm familiar with the evil in some white men, so I'm more prepared than you think. But now I must go back there again, to trade my pelts for supplies. I have stood within their circle of hatred. To me, this return seems the most dangerous part of my journey," she said, shivering with dread.

"No, you must not return there!" Bear Toes said. "The greedy whites will think you have returned for the trapper's furs and the mule. Whoever has ended up with them will not return them to you. You could be killed before you have a chance to explain why you came. It is safer if I trade your furs along with mine. We can't enter the town, but we are allowed to camp in the trees where you hid. Then the white trader comes out to cheat us!" he spat. "Unlike your Cagle, we are at his mercy. If the trader offered him too little, he could enter the hotel or the saloons and find someone who would pay him a better price. We cannot. I won't get much goods for your pelts, but your small bundle will not inconvenience me."

Gratefully Yellow Leaf accepted his offer. She'd had too many frightening nightmares about the town and Cagle's death. So many nights she cried out and awakened trembling and covered with perspiration, just before a shrieking crowd of whites reached her. Sometimes she could not sleep again until she had built a fire and made herb tea. Waiting here with Laughing Eyes was like a reprieve from certain death.

In spite of her impatience, Yellow Leaf enjoyed being with Laughing Eyes during the following days. Both Grazing Fawn and Cagle had been old. She had spent very little time with anyone near her own age. She adored Dancing Squirrel and was intrigued by the mother-daughter relationship. Her dark eyes watched them so intently that Laughing Eyes sensed the other girl's hunger and was deeply touched.

Yellow Leaf thought she might be a mother someday. A gentle and patient one, she hoped, like Laughing Eyes. When the baby was not strapped on her mother's back, or propped against a tree, she swung from a cross pole in her brightly painted and beaded cradleboard. She looked like a snug cocoon, swinging from a silken thread. Laughing Eyes often stopped her work to reach up and start the standing board rocking, which made the baby gurgle with delight. Every few hours she unlaced the thongs so the dimpled nude infant could kick and exercise her arms and legs. Then she would wash off the baby and reline the carrier with clean moss and soft grass. Dancing Squirrel never cried when she was laced in again.

Yellow Leaf marveled at the lack of protest. Dancing Squirrel obviously enjoyed her freedom. Such confinement seemed wrong to her. "I have seen the young of wild animals playing outside their dens and burrows," she said tactfully to Laughing Eyes. "Wild mothers are wise. Spiders, and even some birds can spin or weave, yet none of them bind the limbs of their young."

Laughing Eyes did not get angry. She seemed truly sorry for the ignorance of the younger girl, who had grown up without a mother. "There is a legend that many years ago, men ran on four legs like the fox," she explained. "For some reason, they stood up and began to use only two legs, which were often crooked and ugly from the unaccustomed burden. Then, shortly before her child was born, some forgotten woman dreamed. She saw half a milkweed pod floating on blue water. Inside, snuggled in the fluffy seeds, was a beautiful baby. The pod floated to shore and a youth with strong straight legs stepped out and walked away into the forest. Because of her vision, this mother made the first cradleboard. She lined it with moss and made thongs to hold her baby in. She bore a son, and when he outgrew his snug cradleboard, the other mothers saw his strong back and straight legs. They also began to make them. Infants no longer crawled off bluffs or tumbled into cooking fires. You would not have been lost if you had been younger and still safely strapped to your mother's back," Laughing Eyes pointed out.

Yellow Leaf thought about the legend and the safety factor. She stretched out her legs and examined them. They were straight and well formed. Her back was strong, and her body bore no scars from burns. Love welled up for the unknown mother who had protected her. Laughing Eyes was right. If the sorrowful march had been a year or two earlier, she would not be separated from her family. But then she would not have known Cagle. Would she have wanted to miss that part of her life? Yellow Leaf rested her cheek on her knees and gazed into the flames in the center of the floor. She stiffened as she caught a glimpse of the beautiful woman's face again, with the medallion glinting and swinging. She strained to draw the image closer, then sighed with disappointment as it vanished.

Yellow Leaf resumed her work on the purple and red designs she was weaving around the top of a basket. They had expected Bear Toes and the other man back several days ago. She felt restless at their delay. Perhaps she should have started her journey from the cabin instead of coming here. She could have traded or sold the pelts in some other town along the way. She and Laughing Eyes had been confined to the tepee for two days because of heavy rains. The village was a sea of red mud, and the river had overflowed its banks. With the top flap closed to keep out the rain, the tepee stayed full of smoke. If she stood, it made her eyes sting and stream tears. Yellow Leaf longed for her roomy cabin where she was free to move around, and for the stone fireplace that carried away the smoke.

Laughing Eyes didn't seem to mind, or even notice any discomfort. She had never known any other way of life. If she was worried about her husband's extended absence, she didn't mention it. When a brave went hunting, he might be gone one day or ten; she was used to waiting. She didn't seem to worry either, as Yellow Leaf did, that they had used the last of the deer meat Bear Toes had left.

The next morning dawned clear, although there was still an icy chill in the air. "We must fish today," Laughing Eyes told her, beginning to make preparations.

"It will be time wasted," Yellow Leaf protested. "The water is angry and full of mud. The young boys fish, but nothing is caught."

"I know," Laughing Eyes said, smiling. "Still, we must fish."

Yellow Leaf felt angry and frustrated. Even the smoky tepee was preferable to being out in such weather. "Why does she insist when she knows we can't catch anything?" she muttered. But she dutifully followed along the slippery trail. Dancing Squirrel, strapped to her mother's back, watched Yellow Leaf follow. She dimpled and chortled out loud as the girl jumped back and shivered when a limb slapped and showered her with icy splashes from the leaves.

Their breakfast had been scant. Wild greens they had picked and boiled, with no meat to season them. Yellow Leaf's stomach rumbled with emptiness. Laughing Eyes was nursing a baby. She would need more than greens, or both would be sick. Cagle had taught her to make various kinds of snares for small game. He could make deadly traps with a few bent twigs and bits of cord. When they returned from this useless attempt to fish, she would set some of the traps and nooses in the woods along the river bank.

She was even more baffled when Laughing Eyes made only a halfhearted attempt to catch fish. She built a fire near overhanging bluffs and propped Dancing Squirrel near it. They threw out a few baited hand lines and tied them to the branches of willow trees growing along the bank. Then they sat near the fire. It would be impossible to see a tugging line from here, Yellow Leaf knew, especially with wind blowing the branches. After sitting by the fire for about an hour, Laughing Eyes suggested they take in the lines and return to the village. Then, instead of taking the shortest way back to the tepee, the older girl circled around so they came through the center of the settlement. Laughing Eyes seemed to be laying a snake trail, winding back and forth so that they passed most of the other wigwams. At the slurping sound of each step they took, some of the tent flaps were pulled aside for a moment and then closed.

They had been back in their tepee for a short time when a plump woman entered. She was carrying a dressed squirrel, which she laid near the fire without mentioning it. She chatted about the weather, commented on the beauty of Laughing Eyes' daughter, then left. She was followed by an older woman who brought a piece of venison and complained that her husband had provided more meat than she needed. She hoped Laughing Eyes could use what she had brought so it would not be wasted. Another brought a small bowl of cornmeal. She had ground too much, she said, and was afraid it would go bad in such weather. Laughing Eyes graciously thanked each of them.

Yellow Leaf began to smile. The sham fishing trip had been to let other villagers know they were out of food!

65

By walking through the settlement without a catch, Laughing Eyes had signaled their need, and without sacrificing her pride or dignity. Many tent flaps had been raised. Others would bring food tomorrow, and every day thereafter, until Bear Toes returned.

Three days later the return of the band of men was signaled by shouts of young boys and the excited barking of village dogs. Men from family groups who had recently arrived hurried to ask how much the pelts had brought. A large fire was built in the center of the village, robes were spread, and the men talked. Yellow Leaf and Laughing Eyes helped prepare hot food for the travelers, then they stood back and waited with the other women.

Yellow Leaf tried to be patient, but she was anxious to know which bundle of supplies was hers. Had the trading gone well? She couldn't tell. But she trusted Bear Toes. He would give her exactly what her pelts had brought. He would not expect pay for trading hers, but she had kept out a prime mink skin to give him. It was little enough, she thought, since he had saved her from having to go back to the town where Cagle had died. The trapper had felt strongly about accepting favors, and he had passed the trait on to Yellow Leaf. She would insist that Bear Toes accept the mink so she would leave no unpaid debts behind her.

Later they sat around the fire in the tepee and listened as Bear Toes told about the trip. Bad weather had forced the party to camp in a cave for three days. One man had almost drowned during the crossing of a fast flowing stream. They had rescued him, but his horse and furs had been lost and swept downstream. They had followed for several miles before finding the soaked pelts wedged between boulders. A marauding black bear had invaded their camp one night, and Bear Toes had killed it. He unwrapped the wicked looking claws he had saved for a necklace.

He finally got around to telling about the trading part of his journey, which was what Yellow Leaf was most anxious to hear. "Because our group was the first to arrive this spring, we got more than we expected for our furs," he said proudly. "There are two fur traders in the town now, and both were eager to buy them. The first day they came to our camp, they made very low offers, which angered us. I refused the prices they quoted and told them we had not come so far to be cheated. I told them we would go on to the next town to trade. We could tell they had agreed to offer as little as possible, thinking we would have to accept if they stuck together. Then both would profit. But the second day, when they saw us prepare to leave, they became enemies and began to bid against each other. At sundown we accepted the highest offer, which came from the new trader."

Yellow Leaf did not show her disappointment when Bear Toes proudly gave her the supplies and some coins, but she felt sick. Thinking of how much more Cagle would have received, merely because he was white, made her furious. It was so unfair. Not that it was unexpected. Bear Toes had brought her more than he had warned her to expect. She felt ashamed and ungrateful. The supplies would start her on her journey. She decided not to worry beyond that.

She looked up as more coins clinked and Laughing Eyes gasped. "Don't get excited," her husband teased. "This gold isn't ours. It belongs to Yellow Leaf." He turned the leather pouch inside out to make certain he had emptied it. Some of the gleaming coins were very small and wafer thin.

Yellow Leaf stared in wonder at the small mound of

67

coins. She had never seen so much money! It wasn't possible that it belonged to her. She had already been paid for her pelts.

Bear Toes looked so smug. He was surely teasing Laughing Eyes. The gold was theirs, she decided. But he had brought back many supplies for himself. He could not have gotten so much money besides. Fear swept over her. Surely . . . surely, the band had not attacked and robbed a white traveler! She couldn't conceive of Bear Toes taking part in such a crime, unless they had been provoked. But even if the braves had been attacked, which was possible in or near the wild frontier town, they would surely not have robbed the dead they might have killed in self-defense. Unlike western Indians, who still savagely attacked and killed whites, the people in this area had been beaten into submission too long ago. They would never have returned here, surely! If a crime was committed anywhere in the area, law officials always came to the Indian village. They were the first to be suspected. Bear Toes was not stupid, or did he return to get his family and flee with the gold? A posse could already be headed here. Her face paled and she felt sick.

She stared at Laughing Eyes, who was serenely nursing her baby. She didn't seem upset about the money. Unlike Yellow Leaf, she hadn't thought it might be stolen, or that an angry group of white men could descend and wipe out the entire settlement, which had happened many times. She trembled as she watched Dancing Squirrel's long lashes droop, then lift again as she fought to stay awake. She could think of no honest way to account for so much money. It could bring death to them all!

Bear Toes was puzzled by her lack of enthusiam. He had expected to be bombarded with questions. He had looked forward to surprising her. "Why does so much money make you look miserable? Don't you want to know about it?" he asked.

Yellow Leaf nodded, but she couldn't look at him.

"The sheriff—a different one from the last we met there, who delighted in swaggering around our camp with his big pistols and harassing us—came out to our camp. This lawman, who was not insolent, asked if any of us knew a white trapper named Cagle, or his half-Indian daughter. I was sure he must be the one who defended you, so I finally admitted that I knew you. I told him you were like a sister to my wife, although I did not tell him you were here. This seemed to please him. He said they have found no white family of Cagle's. He gave me this money and asked me to deliver it to you. It is from the sale of the trapper's fine mule. He says there will be more money later, for the pelts, but you must come yourself and sign some papers."

Relief flooded over Yellow Leaf. Bear Toes had not killed nor stolen. The village was safe! But she could hardly believe her good fortune. The traveling judge must have come and decided Cagle's property was legally hers. The white sheriff had not only treated her better than the town's other citizens, he had been honest and sent her the gold. If he had kept it, she would never had known. And Cagle. Even in death he still provided for her. Her heart soared with hope and new confidence. All these omens seemed to foretell good luck.

"Will you wait here with us until the pelts are sold?" Laughing Eyes asked hopefully.

"No! No!" Yellow Leaf cried happily. "I'm not greedy, and I don't want to go back to the town. Not even for so much money. I have already waited much too long. I will leave early tomorrow."

CHAPTER 9

Yellow Leaf's first days on the trail went well. The sun was warm and signs of spring were all around. Wild flowers bloomed along both sides of the game trail she was following, and green leaves fairly burst from every branch. Now that she was actually started on her journey west, she rode slowly, not pushing the horse.

She had not seen another person since leaving the village. There were a few remote farm homes dotted over the area, but she skirted any cleared land. She could have traveled faster on the narrow rutted dirt roads she found, but she decided to stay on the faint trails, where she only risked meeting Indians or a trapper.

She usually stopped near a stream at dusk. Sometimes there was a small cave or an overhanging bluff for shelter. If not, she made a wickiup of poles and covered the frame with branches or dead weeds. When she unrolled her bed furs, the shelter became a cozy den. Even when the temperature dropped, she slept in warm comfort. She was not afraid. Experience had taught her to fear people more than wild creatures. She still had food, but she sometimes took a fish for her supper. She would have to start setting snares soon.

The sun was low, and shafts of golden light penetrated the trees as the horse reached the top of a hill. A large lake stretched as far as she could see. It was a beautiful campsite. She could still travel another hour or two, but she decided to stop here for the night.

She searched until she found the type of fern Grazing Fawn had used for soap. When crushed it made a soapy lather. She bathed in the lake, lathering and rinsing her long hair until it squeaked between her fingers. Her teeth chattered as she ran from the water and was hit by the evening wind. She grabbed up a blanket and warmed near the fire where she had left a stew simmering.

A full moon rose above the wooded hills. Another reflected one seemed to slide across the rippling waves. She wove her damp hair into thick braids and tied them with leather strips. The sun-warmed boulder would hold its heat most of the night. She decided to spread her bed there, with no roof between her and the stars. She felt blissfully happy as she lay gazing into the sky. She thought of Bear Toes and Laughing Eyes and touched the pouch of coins fastened inside her blouse. She had stuffed it with moss so the coins would not clink together.

"If I had yellow hair and blue eyes, I could go right to the middle of a town, give someone the gold, and ride a stage coach all the way," she murmured dreamily. Cagle had told her about the stages drawn by double teams of horses, and how fresh horses were picked up at stations along the way. They fairly flew over the roads, and the passengers were bounced around like walnuts in a basket. She tried to imagine herself traveling in one, then she burst into laughter as she visualized the horror on the faces of other white passengers. "They would walk West rather than ride in comfort with a heathen Injun," she giggled. "So I have enough money to ride, but it's no good because I don't have a light skin!" She snuggled deeper into the furs. She could hear the hobbled horse moving around as he grazed.

Yellow Leaf awoke at dawn and prepared cornmeal mush for breakfast. Birds sang and a large bass splashed to the surface of the lake. She was tempted to linger here for a few days, but she had to take advantage of the good weather. Why hadn't someone settled in such a perfect spot? she wondered. Surely there couldn't be a more beautiful place for a cabin.

She had loaded the horse and was tying on her bedroll when she heard a hard-running horse coming. Before she could grab the lines and hide in the brush, it burst into view. The small boy who was riding so wildly was as startled as Yellow Leaf. He reined in so sharply that his horse reared, and he fell to the ground. The fall knocked the breath out of him. "Are you all right?" Yellow Leaf cried, running to him. Frightened at seeing her, the red-haired boy gasped for air and tried to roll away.

"I'm not going to hurt you. I just wanted to see if you are hurt," Yellow Leaf scolded, stopping.

"Yer—yer an Injun!" the boy stammered as he lay staring up at her. "Yer Injun, but you talk American. What are you doing here on our land?" he blurted.

"I camped here last night, but I didn't know it was your land. I'm sorry," the girl said gravely. "But I'm packed now and ready to leave so you don't have to worry." She mounted the horse and turned toward the trail.

"Wait! Please wait," he called, rising and brushing dust from his trousers. "I need help. Do you know anything about bringing babies?"

"Yes, I do. Why?" Yellow Leaf asked curiously. Grazing Fawn was much in demand by prospective mothers. She had delivered more babies than she could count. And Yellow Leaf had always accompanied her during the summers, often to other villages. During that last year, after the Indian woman had grown so feeble,

72

Yellow Leaf had delivered a dozen or more infants alone, following instructions from the old woman.

"It's my Maw," the boy said fearfully. "The baby's coming early, and my Paw's away on a barge trip. I don't know what to do so I started for Nelson's place, but it's fifteen miles away. Will you come?"

Yellow Leaf started to refuse. "Why should I go out of my way to deliver a white baby?" she thought rebelliously. "She might not even let me in the house when I get there!" It wasn't, however, just the pleading look in the eyes of the boy that made her change her mind. She thought of the woman, alone and needing help. Suddenly her color didn't matter. She couldn't just turn and ride away. "Let's go," she sighed. "Show me the way."

The boy introduced himself as Jeb Tompkins. She followed him around the lake and three miles through the forest, to a log house nestled in a long, flat meadow surrounded by low hills. There was only one large room, similar to Cagle's. It had a kitchen at one end, and two double beds were in the other. There was a half-loft that extended out across the ceiling, and a wood ladder nailed against the wall led up to it. It was probably where the boy slept.

A pale red-haired woman was lying on one of the beds. Her eyes widened in panic as she saw Yellow Leaf follow her son into the room. She looked at the two little girls, also red-haired, asleep in the bed across from her. She struggled to get up. Then she sagged back helplessly and bit her lips to keep from crying out.

"Don't be afraid of her, Maw," Jeb said. "I found her camped down at the big boulders by the lake. She only came because I begged her to. She knows all about babies. She's brought lots of 'em."

Yellow Leaf smiled reassuringly at the woman. "I can

73

see that there isn't as much rush as Jeb thought. I'm on my way west and have a long way to go. Would you rather have your son ride for your nearest neighbor? I won't mind if you would rather have a white woman's help."

"You speak English!" the woman said, losing some of her fear. "No. Please stay," she whispered. Her face tightened with pain. "I—I always have a bad time," she said apologetically.

Yellow Leaf nodded. Jeb woke his sisters and dressed them while she prepared their breakfast. While they were eating, she went out to the horse and brought in her packet of herbs. Selecting a tiny bundle, she brewed tea and took it to the woman, who had watched anxiously as the Indian girl moved back and forth. Mrs. Tompkins had watched her sort through the dried herbs, and she was frightened again. Suspicious, she shook her head and refused to drink the greenish looking liquid. The girl was a savage, after all. Why wouldn't she take an opportunity to strike back at whites if she got a chance? Panic filled her eyes again. The herb could be a deadly poison!

As she watched Mrs. Tompkins, Yellow Leaf could almost read her thoughts. She stiffened with resentment. "I came here to help, not harm you or your children," she told her. "You said you always have a difficult birth. My herb will make you dreamy and relaxed. The baby will be healthy, and you will hardly know when it arrives." She took the thin white hand in her dark one and told her about Grazing Fawn, who had taught her about herbs, and how many illnesses could be cured or helped by the natural medicines she carried. "But I won't insist if you are still afraid to drink it," she added.

"I'm sorry," Mrs. Tompkins apologized. "I do trust you. I'll drink it." She sipped cautiously when Yellow Leaf lifted her a little and held the mug to her lips. She had expected some horrible bitter taste; instead the brew had a pleasant mint flavor, along with another she couldn't identify. It had a pungent, acrid smell. Hoping that her faith in the girl wasn't misguided, she drank it all and lay back on the straw pillow.

The drowsiness slipped up on her almost immediately. She was aware of everything but she seemed to be floating a little above the bed. She watched Jeb take his sisters outside to play, at the Indian girl's suggestion. He was prepared to stay if necessary, but his relief was evident when Yellow Leaf assured him that she would need no help. "He's brave. Like his father," she thought proudly.

It seemed only a few minutes later that Yellow Leaf was placing the baby in her arms. "Here, Mrs. Tompkins, take this fine warrior," she said, smiling down at the bewildered new mother. Dazed, the woman stared at the baby, then at the copper-colored face she had feared. The girls were squealing their delight at the new arrival. Jeb was pale with awe.

"A boy! That's what we wanted this time. To even things out," Mrs. Tompkins whispered huskily as she blinked back tears of happiness. "I want you to name him," she added as she clasped Yellow Leaf's hand.

"Cagle. Cagle Tompkins," the girl said without hesitation.

"Cagle it is, then," the woman agreed, holding him closer.

Jeb started giggling. "What if she'd said Gray Wolf, Running Bear, or White Fox — an Indian name?" he asked mischievously.

"Then that would have been your new brother's name, young man!" his mother said tartly. "Don't you think I considered that possibility before I offered?" She looked startled, then smiled when Yellow Leaf began to giggle

75

too. Somehow the Indian girl couldn't visualize the tiny red-faced and red-headed infant with a name like Running Bear.

Yellow Leaf stayed with the family for three more days, but they still begged her not to leave. Her presence had brightened up their lives. Even Jeb, who considered himself too old for listening to bedtime stories, was caught up in the legends she told the little girls. He was too literal minded to believe that a terrible drouth, which had laid waste to the land many years ago, could have been broken because some ancient Indian chief braved attacking eagles to climb up to the top of a mountain and shoot heavy rainfilled clouds with arrows. But it seemed almost plausible with the girl telling the story in front of the fireplace at night. Animals were as individual from one another as people to Yellow Leaf, which gave him new thoughts to consider. Each species had its heroes, weaklings, good or evil characters in the tales she told. Although he believed otters had always been expert swimmers, spiders were created knowing how to spin webs, and beavers were just naturally meant to be dam builders, the fanciful myths about how and why the first was supposed to have learned was still fascinating.

Jeb had never intended to be anything but a farmer, like his father, but now he began to make notes as the Indian girl told her stories. Some day he might make them into a book for children. The legends were a bridge back through time, probably as old as the red race. They should be preserved. For the first time Jeb began to dream of being an author. Years later Jeb would look back with gratitude to the young Indian girl who had first made him aware of the spellbinding power of words.

When the family saw that Yellow Leaf was determined to resume her journey, Mrs. Tompkins replenished her food supply with meat from their smokehouse, and added dried beans, corn, and fruit. Yellow Leaf worried about a wide river Jeb told her she would have to cross. It was a mighty stream at any time, but it would be even wider now because of flooding. "There's no use going up- or downriver," he warned. "There's no place narrow enough to ford, and no horse is strong enough to swim it when it's this high. There's a ferryboat, and that's the only way to cross."

Cagle had mentioned such a river, but Yellow Leaf had forgotten about it. When she grew tense and quiet with worry, Jeb couldn't understand why she was so upset. "All you do is lead your horse onto the boat, pay the man, and ride across. Are you afraid of boats? Or don't you have any money?" he asked.

"I have money, and I'm not afraid of the boat," Yellow Leaf sighed. "But what seems so simple for you will probably be very difficult — even impossible — for me. The boat owner may refuse to take me at any price. Even if he should be willing, other passengers will refuse to go across if he takes me aboard. They will be angry or afraid . . ."

Jeb and Mrs. Tompkins hadn't thought of that, but they knew she had reason to worry. They had been afraid of her too at first, because they had judged her by outward appearance. They felt ashamed as they remembered the fear and mistrust. For the first time they considered the difficulties of being an Indian — of being in constant conflict with the fear and hatred of almost any white person she met. How brave she was to attempt such a long journey! Like Bear Toes, Mrs. Tompkins felt the trip was possibly suicidal. Her heart was heavy with dread as she and Jeb watched the girl ride away. "We'll never see her again. And we'll never know how the story ends," Jeb thought. "She could be shot down for a savage in some western town, or kidnapped by some warrior from another tribe

77

and taken off for his bride . . . She could join and lead an uprising against cruel whites who killed a bunch of Indians and set fire to their village." During the winter he would write a story about Yellow Leaf, but it would have a happy ending, he decided.

CHAPTER 10

The forest was too dense for easy travel, so Yellow Leaf was forced to follow the road. She stopped often to listen for approaching horses. She had to dismount several times and lead her horse into the trees. Two wagons and teams had gone by. One was a farm wagon loaded with firewood. The other was a huge wagon covered with flapping canvas and pulled by a team of oxen. A stout blond couple sat in the front seat. The back was filled with household goods and children. "A Conestoga!" Yellow Leaf gasped in delight. Cagle had described them, but it was the first she had ever seen. "They're settlers, heading west — possibly near where I'm going," she thought enviously. There was even a crate of chickens tied on the back. The wagon was truly like a home on wheels!

All the traffic made Yellow Leaf uneasy, so she stayed in the trees, trying to pass both wagons and hoping to take the road again later. She left the big wagon behind but she worried about catching up with the other wagon and riders she had seen. She was still in the trees when she saw water glinting in the distance. She had reached the river. She caught her breath. Jeb's description hadn't prepared her for the sight. The swiftly moving water looked like flowing mud, and it was surely more than a mile across!

A large flatboat made of timbers was crossing from the other side. A group of men, stripped to the waist, were fighting the current with long oars and poles. Three horses and riders were waiting patiently at the landing, and the first wagon was lumbering into position behind them. When the boat docked, the crew laid heavy planks to shore. The passengers from the other side crossed them to dry land and rode past her hiding place. Yellow Leaf was terrified of such a mighty stream, and her stomach tightened with the familiar dread associated with meeting strange whites. She felt uneasy and miserable. If only there was another way to cross, but Jeb had said there wasn't.

She decided to watch a crossing before she approached the ferry. Maybe there would be fewer whites waiting on the next trip. She remained hidden and watched the riders lead their horses aboard and tether them to iron rings on the deck. If they panicked they wouldn't jump overboard. It took some time to load the wagon of firewood. The horses were skittish and refused to cross the sagging planks. Their owner cursed and lashed out with his whip, but to no avail. Yellow Leaf was outraged at his brutality. Why didn't he try soothing the frightened animals? The furious man finally left his seat and blindfolded the horses. Then he enlisted the aid of the crew and other passengers to push and drag them across to the deck.

Yellow Leaf had started eating the lunch Mrs. Tompkins had given her. She stopped chewing and held her breath as the wagon and team crossed. She half expected the boat to sink under the weight, but it only shivered and settled a little deeper into the water. Her eyes grew round and she tensed as ropes were cast off and the straining crew again worked with the long poles, then the oars. She was afraid the clumsy craft might swirl off downstream like a floating leaf, but the men handled the ferry expertly. She watched with admiration as they pitted their strength against the strong waters.

She had thought it might take hours to cross, but the

ferry was back again before the Conestoga wagon arrived. After the passengers had ridden off, Yellow Leaf mounted her horse and slowly rode down toward the shore. The crew was having lunch and resting in the shade of tall cottonwood trees. They stood up and watched apprehensively as she approached. Yellow Leaf's heart began to pound with fear. "They won't take me across. They won't let me on the boat," she thought.

"Looky here, boys. We got ourselves a real live Injun! A little squaw!" one snickered insolently.

"Shut yer mouth, Gabe!" his boss said tensely. His sharp eyes searched the trees on the slope above them. "Where thar's one Injun, there's likely to be a big passel of 'em. Unless yer anxious to lose yore hair, don't nobody make a move till we kin make out what she wants. You git smart and yer liable to be eatin' a fire arrow!"

Yellow Leaf stayed on her horse, ready to flee if any of them approached. "I have money to pay. I want to cross on your boat," she said, surprised that her voice sounded so confident. Her perfect English seemed to confuse them. The tense man moved forward, then stopped as Yellow Leaf backed her horse. Taking advantage of his indecision, she looked up toward the forest and raised both arms in a signal, bringing her hand back from a sweeping gesture to point at the man. "Uh . . . how many of you wuz wantin' to cross?" he asked uneasily, still looking up.

"I'll cross first, alone, to make sure it's safe. Then the others will come in two groups, in case you try to trick us, which wouldn't be wise," the girl said softly. She stared back at him defiantly, not hiding her dislike. Like all whites, he had forced her to lie, which she resented.

"Uh . . . well, I never took no Injuns onto my boat before. I dunno. My crew ain't goin' to like it . . ." the man hedged. The men nodded, but they looked afraid. None of

81

them were armed and the large flatboat seemed to shrink when they thought about being mid-river and helpless, with a group of unruly savages aboard.

"Oh, you'll take me," Yellow Leaf insisted confidently, although she was quaking inside. "And then you'll bring the others over. The river is too high for us to ford." She didn't look around as squeaking wheels signaled the approach of the covered wagon. Why couldn't they have come after the ferry had pulled away? The family of whites was sure to complicate everything for her.

"These other white folks ain't likely to want to make a crossing with you aboard. I got to get along with my customers. There's another ferry about twenty-five miles upriver. Why don't you go there?" the man asked bluntly.

"No! My people will cross here! You don't seem to understand that none of you have a choice," Yellow Leaf said coldly. "I'm crossing over first. You explain to the people in the wagon. I think they will choose to go with me rather than with either group from my tribe. If they prefer to ride across alone, let them wait!" She looked up at the forest and made another sweeping motion from the land to the boat, then she rode forward.

The crew had grouped together in front of the planks that bridged the few feet of water between the end of the boat and the riverbank. They looked sullen, but their leader's hissing reminder that an unknown number of hostile eyes were watching made them step aside. The horse gave her no trouble. He crossed the planks as though he had been boarding ferryboats all his life. Yellow Leaf dismounted and tethered him to a ring at the far end of the deck — the prow, she supposed, although both ends looked the same.

Now that she was aboard and dreading the ride, Yellow Leaf was anxious to get started. The boat swayed just enough to make her stomach feel uneasy. She wished she had waited to eat lunch. The leader seemed to be having trouble with the couple in the wagon. She slipped back toward the mooring ropes and stopped, apparently only gazing down into the muddy water. She had no difficulty overhearing the conversation with her keen ears.

"You kin do as you please," the ferryman said. "I don't blame you none fer not wantin' to ride over with an Injun on account of yer children, but it might be worse if you stay here alone. She says thar's fifty or more of her people in the woods up yonder. ("The liar!" Yellow Leaf thought contemptuously. She had mentioned no number, and it was he who had first planted the idea that she was traveling with a large party. She had only gone along with it, hoping to cross safely. But now the men's imagination had turned the invisible Indians into a bloodthirsty war party, in paints and wielding tomahawks!) "They're afeard of the boat so they sent her to try it first," he continued. "The tribe's gonna watch, and if she makes it, they'll all come down."

"It's *your* ferry. Surely you have the right to refuse service to heathens. Don't you?" the plump woman said disdainfully. She spoke with a heavy accent and eyed Yellow Leaf with distaste, more than with fear.

Her husband and the boat owner stared at her. "Be reasonable, Greta," her husband said. "If he refuses to take the girl, all the Indians could sweep down that hill, kill all of us, and steal the ferry!" Suddenly his face lit up. "I've got a gun in the wagon, all loaded and ready to fire. We could load up, then order her ashore and hold her off until the boat is well out in the water. We would be gone before her tribe could get down here . . ."

His voice trailed off as Yellow Leaf gathered up her long fringed skirt and left the boat. "Hand me the gun until we reach the other side," she ordered. The man paled and began to grope behind the seat. He grasped it and started to hand it out. "Butt first!" Yellow Leaf warned, her eyes icy. He hastily turned the muzzle upward and gingerly handed it down.

"My people are growing impatient. Leave them here. You must take me now!" she told the leader, who was now arguing with his rebellious crew.

She heard him tell them that they would cross and then stay on the other bank and tie up for the night. They would not return for the large band of Indians. This plot seemed to satisfy the men. By now they were all so jumpy that they were seeing fierce red faces behind every tree.

After a whispered warning about their plans, and that they would be stranded here, the white couple was anxious to go on the same boat with the Indian girl. The woman stood on the deck, her children huddled around her, and glared at Yellow Leaf as the oxen and wagon were driven on deck.

Yellow Leaf ignored her. She sighed and sat down cross-legged to watch. She kept her back to the other shore so none of them could sneak up on her. The gun across her lap should make them keep their distance. How complicated her copper skin, Indian dress, and necklaces had made what should have been a routine crossing of the river! She had lost almost three hours of traveling time for no reason. What was worse, she had been forced to threaten and frighten them, even the wide-eyed children.

But the two older ones weren't very frightened of her. She smiled as they sneaked around the wagon away from their mother. Both had yellow hair and light eyes as blue as a summer sky. They were plump like their parents, with rosy cheeks that looked painted. They were more curious than afraid of her. "You're the first real live Injun we've seen," the boy whispered. "Have you ever scalped anybody?" he blurted. The younger girl held back, peering around her brother.

"No. Not yet!" Yellow Leaf whispered back, trying to look fierce, so they would rush back to their mother before she caught and punished them.

The boy looked disappointed, but the girl seemed relieved. They both jumped and retreated as the woman swept around the wagon. She slapped the boy and dragged the girl away, berating them in a strange guttural language as she glared threateningly at Yellow Leaf. The Indian girl stared back at her without moving, but she was disappointed. They were beautiful children, and she was curious about where they were going and where they had come from. Talking with them would have made the trip go faster and kept her mind off the dangerous water.

Yellow Leaf wasn't sure she believed in river demons, but she had been steeped in legends about them. The Indians usually made some offering before venturing to cross on wide or wild waters. Her neck felt shivery as she watched the muddy water tear at the craft. They were hardly halfway across, and the men had to fight desperately to keep from being flung downstream. They didn't seem aware of her now.

The deck had seemed so large while the boat was moored; now it seemed very small and fragile. It quivered under the slap of waves and bucked like a horse. Men were bound to land, and fish to water. Even if there were no demons, each risked disaster when they left their own environment and invaded the other, Yellow Leaf decided fearfully, as she yearned for the feel of dry land.

Her roving dark eyes spotted danger before the others, perhaps because she was expecting it. "The tree! The tree!" she shouted, pointing. A huge tree, with massive roots as tall as the cabin, was being tumbled and rolled directly in their path. The crew redoubled their rowing efforts, hoping to pass in front of it and then to watch it brush by. They almost made it. The large trunk cleared them, but the roots hit the rear of the deck with a jarring crash, turning the front of the boat upstream. Then it rolled over like a playful puppy and slid past. "We made it! Turn Her nose back toward shore. Get her lined up!" the owner yelled.

Only Yellow Leaf had seen the boy pitched overboard at the impact. She shouted another warning and the mother began to scream her terror as she saw the boy drifting away, following the path of the tree. The father's face was pallid as he struggled to remove his heavy boots. He would never make it in time! The boy had already gone under twice. He didn't know how to swim!

Despite her fears, Yellow Leaf dove cleanly and began to swim like an otter. She was within arm's length of the blond head when the boy went under again. This time he failed to come up. The girl dove under water, strong legs churning as she circled and groped. It was impossible to see in the dark water. Her lungs felt as though they would burst. She would have to give up! Suddenly her hand touched cloth. She grabbed for a stronger hold on the shirt, and they popped to the surface. The crew had thrown out anchors and several long trailing ropes the current carried down, then they fought to keep the boat from drifting on top of the children. As hard as she swam, Yellow Leaf could not approach the deck. Just as she was about to give up and let the current take them downstream, where they might land on a sand bar, one of the ropes snaked near enough to grasp. The crew stayed at their oars as the ferry owner and the boy's father reeled them in like fish.

"He's not breathing. He's gone! My son is dead!" the father mourned hopelessly.

"No! No, we can't give up yet!" Yellow Leaf cried, pushing the man aside. She had worked too hard to save the boy; she would not surrender him to the river demons so easily. She turned the child on his stomach and put all her force on his back. Water gushed out of his nose and mouth at each push. When it stopped, she turned him on his back and blew breath into his lungs as she had seen the Indians do. Not that it always worked! Just when she decided she had lost the battle, the boy began to retch and drag in sobbing breaths. Yellow Leaf collapsed on the deck, a sodden heap of fatigue, unnoticed by the happy parents or the jubilant men.

The impatient people waiting on the shore had not been able to see what all the excitement was about. They grumbled at the delay and watched curiously as the drenched Indian girl was wrapped in a warm blanket and placed in the wagon with white children! "I'd as soon take a rattlesnake into my house!" one man sneered. He spat a stream of tobacco juice, then wiped a dirty sleeve across his stained beard.

The stocky blond mother, who had been hovering over Yellow Leaf and murmuring her thanks in a mixture of English and German, turned on the surprised man. Her blue eyes blazed with fury and she advanced on him shouting a scathing stream of German. She was a large woman and formidable in her rage. The man fell silent and retreated, his face crimson at the humiliation of insults he couldn't understand. The other men roared with laughter as the mother shook her finger in the man's face until she was dragged away by her husband.

The bonejarring jolts awakened Yellow Leaf as the oxen plodded to the riverbank. She sighed and opened her eyes when she heard the ferry owner explain that there would be no more crossings until the next day. The dismay of the waiting passengers lessened as he explained that the forest was alive with "redskins" waiting for the boat to return.

The entire episode had been a nightmare for Yellow Leaf. For a moment she was tempted to remain silent. Then she remembered that travelers on both sides of the river would be delayed for no reason, and some of the crossings might be very important. Also, the crew would lose half a day's pay. Weakly she pulled the blanket more tightly around her and descended from the wagon.

"There are no Indians over there," she told the shocked boat owner after she had called him aside. "It's safe to take them across. I'm traveling alone."

The man's jaw sagged. "No Injuns?" he asked in disbelief. "You mean yore story was jest a pack of lies?"

"*Your* lies, Mister. Not mine!" Yellow Leaf said with dignity. "It was you who told the crew that where there was one Indian, there would be a whole passel of them. I just went along with it because I could see that you weren't going to bring me across."

"You've made a danged fool out of me for life!" the man fumed. "What kin I tell my crew and passengers? They'll never let me live it down—that I was skeered witless by one Injun gal. People will still be callin' me 'Injun' Zacharia when I'm so old I can't crawl across my deck!"

How Cagle would have delighted in the situation! He would have whooped with laughter and slapped his thighs at the bigoted man's discomfort.

"The others don't have to know. I ought to let you stew in your own juice but I'll fix it so your pride won't be hurt," Yellow Leaf said, but she couldn't keep from grinning impishly at the angry white man. The grumbling group fell silent as the ferryman followed her down to the water. She faced the trees so far across the reddish yellow water and began to make complicated looking hand signals. She waited, then signaled again. She struggled to keep her face straight as she ignored the other men and talked to the owner of the boat. "I've told my people that your boat is dangerous. My chief has decided to take the tribe away until the river drops. They will be gone by the time you cross." The sheepish looking man nodded.

"I didn't see nothin' over there. Maybe she's lying," one of the crewmen said.

"You white people are too blind to see anything. Most of you can't see past your own feet because you don't know how to use your eyes!" Yellow Leaf retorted.

"I saw an Injun pony and two braves," the dirty man insisted. "One looked like a chief. Then they moved back in the trees and I lost sight of 'em."

"I saw the pony too," another said. "Saw it plain as day. It was white with black spots on its flanks."

The leader of the crew grinned as the men argued about who had seen the most Indians and horses. Yellow Leaf picked up her horse's reins, then stopped and turned back to him. "Mrs. Tompkins said she and her husband were friends of yours. I delivered her new baby and then stayed at their place for several days. She told me to tell you she would skin you alive if you refused to take me across the river. Would it have made any difference if I'd had time to tell you that?"

The man looked down at his boots, then away at the river. "No. I don't reckon it would have," he admitted honestly. "I'd have thought it was some slick Injun lie. I'd have took my men and rid over there expectin' to find them dead and scalped. No . . . if I coulda helped it, I guess you'd never have got aboard my boat. Right or wrong, I . . . all us white folks is jest plain afraid of you Injuns."

Yellow Leaf nodded bleakly and mounted her horse. The man's answer made her sad but it didn't surprise her. It only confirmed what she thought. Wherever she met whites, she would be forced to lie, cheat, outwit, or bluff them, to make her trip safely. Why? she wondered. Cagle had loved her. The Tompkins family were good friends who had begged her to stay with them. Then she thought about her own fear and mistrust of all white people. It seemed to be an instinctive thing, but it had been intensified by her contacts with them. "Maybe we're not meant to be friends except on a one-to-one basis," she decided, "and only after we overcome our mutual distrust." And man seemed to be the only animal she knew of that let color make such a difference.

CHAPTER 11

Yellow Leaf looked up and saw the heavy wagon stopped at the top of the hill. She thought the family was probably waiting for the return of their blanket, so she took it off and folded it as she rode. She shivered in the cool breeze off the river. Her wet hair and clothing made it seem icy.

"No. No. Put the blanket back on. You'll take your death!" the German woman scolded when she rode up to hand it back. "We waited to ask you to travel along with us today. We will stop and have supper in about an hour. Will you eat with us?"

Yellow Leaf was pleased by the unexpected invitation, and so were the children when she shyly accepted. She dropped in behind the wagon, and the older boy and girl filled the half circle of canvas. They chattered like magpies and also asked a lot of questions. Their family name was Schmidt. Karl and Greta were the parents. The boy was also named Karl; his sister was Frieda. The three smaller children, the youngest with scabbed and draining sore eyes, smiled too, but they ducked their heads and were too shy to talk to her.

Later she was so stuffed with supper that she almost fell asleep as they sat around the campfire. Mrs. Schmidt was an excellent cook, but the food was too heavy and rich to suit Yellow Leaf's taste. No wonder they were all so plump, she thought. The woman had kept forcing more food on her long after she would have liked to stop eating.

"You're so thin, so thin," she fretted. "You need lots of good nourishing food or you'll get sick."

Yellow Leaf was touched by her concern, but it was time wasted when she tried to explain that she was not skinny by Indian standards. The difference was that her diet was mostly meat and greens. "No! It's not healthy. You need more flesh on your poor little bones," the blond woman still insisted. Yellow Leaf smiled and nodded.

After the younger children were put to sleep inside the wagon, two beds were spread under it for the man and woman and the older boy and girl. Then they and Yellow Leaf exchanged information about where they were headed. The German family would be joining a wagon train at a fort about 200 miles away, for the long journey west.

Tears came to the motherly woman's eyes as Yellow Leaf told about her own quest, which might be fruitless. She didn't notice the tears as she gazed into the fire and talked about the forced roundup of her people and how she was lost. Her face softened as she told about Cagle and her life with him. Then it tightened with pain when she described his death, her hard winter alone, and the time spent with Bear Toes and Laughing Eyes. "I'm on my way at last, but I don't know where I'm going," she finished smiling.

The blond woman was visibly upset. She moaned in German and her husband tried to comfort her. Yellow Leaf was bewildered by her anguish until she switched back to English. "It was an opportunity for a new and better life that drew us here, where rich farmland is free for the taking. We gave no thought to the Indian people the land belonged to—ignorant, filthy, and savage killers, we were told. But you are not like that. You risked your own life to save our son. We've come to steal your country too, but we didn't understand. We didn't know. Please forgive us. I'm sorry—so sorry," she wept.

Yellow Leaf felt confused. She had not thought of the Schmidt family as personal enemies, or thieves coming to take her land. Yet it was true. And she would have fought them fiercely if they had tried to take away her cabin. The problem was too big and complicated. Her people were homeless because too many Schmidts had come, but it was too late. Even if this one family returned to Germany, it wouldn't reverse things or return the land. The Indians were a defeated people. There was no hope that their condition would ever be improved.

She felt concern as the woman fervently vowed to treat Indians with respect and kindness from now on. Her family would remember that they were the only true natives of this beautiful land; a proud people who had been made homeless by guests they had welcomed. "By knowing you, I feel differently about all Indians now," she said.

"You and your family can be slain if you start thinking all Indians are like me," Yellow Leaf said bluntly. "They aren't. Like whites, many of my people are evil and not to be trusted. They kill each other in wars and there are many bloodthirsty savages, as the whites claim. Some attack the settlers and wagon trains only because they are afraid of losing their hunting grounds. They don't realize how many whites have come, so they think if they drive back or kill this one group, their trouble will be over. I'm sorry to admit it, but there are others who kill for the joy of killing. The fierce western Indians have not been beaten down by civilization. I would be no safer among them than you would. You will be wise to forget about me and be careful where you place your trust."

Although her words were true, Yellow Leaf felt sick, and like a traitor to her own people. After all she had suffered at the hands of white people, she had just advised these to treat all Indians with the same fear and dislike they had shown when they first met her at the river. But her warning was necessary if they were to survive the trip west. She stood up and slipped away to her bed of furs at the edge of the forest.

During the following days Yellow Leaf and the Schmidts traveled together. The oxen and cumbersome wagon were slow, but she wanted to spare the horse, so she didn't mind. They had all grown fond of each other, despite certain problems. Mrs. Schmidt still felt hurt that the girl preferred to hunt and prepare her own food, but she no longer insisted that the Indian girl share their meals.

After traveling a long, tiring day the girl withdrew into the forest and returned rested and refreshed. Somehow the forest seemed to be her church. How or why, the German couple couldn't understand. The hoot of an owl made her tense with fright and foreboding. She would stop immediately, pull away a layer of dry leaves, draw mysterious symbols in moist earth, and then cover the spot. Her darting black eyes saw so many things they would have missed if she had not pointed them out. She would lead the children to a shrub that looked no different than others, and part it gently so they could marvel at a tiny nest with eggs no larger than beads. How could she know a nest would be there? She could seem so mature for her age and then revert to such childish delight at the sight of blooming wild flowers or the dipping flight of a redbird.

"She seems so much a part of all this," Mrs. Schmidt murmured in German. "Her very heart seems to throb in tune with all the wild things. The sight of a single dead bird saddens her like a personal loss, yet there are thousands and thousands of living ones. I don't understand, but I feel sad to watch her. I wish this lovely land had not been discovered by white people. It should have remained theirs."

"I feel it too," Karl said. "She's so different from us, and yet a white man reared her. If this Cagle tried to turn her into a white child, he failed. Perhaps it's because he had no wife to mother her that she's still so Indian."

"I'm glad he failed," his wife retorted. "I've been so worried about sickness on our trip, but she has prepared herbs and medicine to deal with almost any illness. And they work! Look how quickly her salve cured the baby's eyes!" she marveled. "He's suffered so much, and it lasted so long. I was afraid the infection would eventually blind him. And Frieda's high fever. A few dry leaves crumbled in syrup and it was gone in an hour! A doctor couldn't have done as well. It's incredible how wise she is about curing sickness. She heals it so easily with a bit of moss, with bark, root, or leaves from some common plant growing beside the road. How I envy her knowledge."

Along with the good things, there were drawbacks to traveling with the Indian girl, they had discovered. There were the slights and outright hostility they encountered each time their paths crossed that of other white people. One glimpse of the dusky face and jet black braids, and any sign of friendliness vanished. In one small settlement, where they stopped to buy flour, lard, and sugar, the clerk refused to sell to them even though Yellow Leaf had not entered the store. They had left the town with taunts and insults ringing in their ears. Their frightened and bewildered children had hugged the floor of the wagon as stones were hurled and bounced off the canvas top. Adults stood along the main street watching, but none stepped out to reprimand the youths who flung rocks.

Yellow Leaf had wanted to circle the town and join

95

them on the other side. She had tried to warn them that her presence could endanger them, but they hadn't believed such a cruel thing could happen. The forceful German woman had refused to consider allowing her to leave them and circle the town like some wild animal. She thought her white family would protect the girl, even if the residents didn't relish the short stop of an Indian in their town. She had been wrong.

When they stopped outside the town, blood was streaming from a deep gash on Yellow Leaf's leg. Her dark eyes were stricken and full of remembered shock and pain. "No! No! Stay away from me. I tried to warn you!" she spat out when Mrs. Schmidt rushed toward her. She darted away into the trees. The German family waited silently, not knowing what else to do. When the girl returned, she was calm and friendly again. A length of vine held wet leaves over the wound, which she didn't mention. She seemed to have forgotten the frightening incident.

That night, however, Yellow Leaf sat tossing stones into a winding brook. She had decided to leave the Schmidts — for their own good. They talked so eagerly about the wagon train, but she knew her presence would cause the other white people to refuse to let them join the group of new settlers. They were loyal and probably foolish enough to refuse to ask her to leave them. Rather than hurt her, they might even attempt the trip alone, as stubborn as Mrs. Schmidt was. It would be certain death. Besides the hostile Indians there would be a desert, and snow in high mountains after she left them to head farther south where the tribes had been relocated. Since she would not be going all the way with them, it was better to leave them now. Travelers were forced to join together for safety, and hire guides and scouts to lead them. The Schmidts might not find another train to join. Would the white

family make the journey safely, even in a group? Cagle had said the trails west were outlined in graves, burned Conestoga wagons, and bleached bones.

How silly she was to have dreamed of the excitement of the wagon train, and the vain hope that the white family's acceptance of her might make a difference! Her low bitter laugh was more like a sob as she rested her head on her knees. They were all heading the same direction, and she wanted to stay with the Schmidts. They also wanted her, but now they surely realized how much trouble she could bring them. "I'm the one who knew it was impossible. Why do I keep forcing white people to mistreat me and remind me of my race?"

When she was certain all the family was asleep, Yellow Leaf rose, packed her horse, and slipped away. She had taught little Karl and Frieda to read her symbols. They would see her picture drawing, sketched where she had spread her bed, and the family would know that she would not return. She would miss them — especially the children. But she would get accustomed to being alone again. She always had. Perhaps she should be grateful for the taunts and the stones, even her wound. "Injun! Injun! Injun!" she chanted wearily. The horse hesitated and twitched his ears, then plodded on when he decided the chant was not a command to stop or change directions.

CHAPTER 12

Several weeks later, when Yellow Leaf reached the Indian Territory, she discovered that the removed Indians were scattered over hundreds of miles. There was no specific place with records, where she could ask for help. She roved the country like a gypsy, from one settlement to another, asking questions and leaving information about herself. The people moved around within the limits of the Territory, so she often traveled for days only to find herself in a village she had already checked weeks before and in another section. Even if she'd had the names of her parents, it would have been of little or no help. Indian names were mostly taken from nature and were too similar. There were dozens of braves named after the same birds and animals, with no way to distinguish one from another. There might be a chief named Gray Eagle in one place, and a newborn infant with the same name only a few miles away.

The climate was blistering hot, the land as dry and arid as a desert in places, although the people said the winters were terrible. Yellow Leaf grew more and more discouraged. She should have listened to Bear Toes and others who had tried to dissuade her. She had embarked on a hopeless quest.

One evening she led her horse down a treeless slope to a large village beside a stream that was white with foaming rapids. It was exactly like the dozens of others she had visited, but prettier because of the small river. She had grown to detest the flat desolate land, with mile after mile of treeless plains. She was homesick for the cool green mountains back east. She did not want to be trapped here when the weather turned bitter cold and the snows blew level with the land, and no hills to stop it. Many horses and cattle died every winter, and the people suffered terribly. "We're going back home," she whispered tiredly, patting the weary horse. "I know now that the search was hopeless from the start. I never should have tried. My family must have died on the march. Others fled and went back east. Somehow my family would have escaped and returned to look for me."

She dreaded entering the village. Many children had been lost. Besides her own disappointment, she had raised and then dashed the wild hopes of many Indian families who thought she might be their lost child. She had found the Indians depressed, apathetic, and homesick. The spirit had been taken out of them. Only the young had begun to adapt to this land, because they could not remember freedom or any other home. Some still talked of returning to the mountains and home, but they were afraid of the white soldiers. The old ones only waited impatiently for the release of death.

Most of the families had not received the free land and goods they had been promised when they arrived here. The government's final betrayal had taken the heart out of her people. They had been placed on land that already belonged to other more warlike tribes who resented them. They were trapped between the Army and unfriendly red men, with white settlers overrunning the country. There was no place for them. Yellow Leaf became frightened when she recalled Bear Toes' warning. If she stayed here, she would be trapped too, or scooped up and confined to a reservation. She had no way to prove she had not been among those who had been driven here. She decided it was time to return to Cagle's cabin. She was young and strong; she could support herself and have a good life. Someday she would find a brave with spirit and be a good wife. There would be children — her own family.

When Yellow Leaf entered the village, she asked for Mountain Bird's tepee. She had been told this woman had lost a child on the march. But she had no optimistic hopes. She had followed too many false leads to disappointment. The information that led her here was even more skimpy than usual. The sad and toothless old woman who sent her to this settlement had not known the age or even the sex of the lost child. She only knew this mother had mourned a dead or lost child and survived the march.

Since she had decided to go back, Yellow Leaf thought she would check this last village and then start the long return journey. She would not look back with regret. She had made the search and failed. While she had lived mostly off the land, she had spent all the money Bear Toes had received along with supplies for her pelts. But she had not touched the gold coins in the pouch. She dreaded the long trip, but the hidden gold gave her courage.

There was a youth sitting in front of Mountain Bird's home. Strong muscles rippled under his shirt as he polished the curved wood of a new bow. He glanced over his shoulder as Yellow Leaf approached. The reins dropped from her nerveless hand. Her body went rigid with shock and her breath felt smothered. He rose slowly and stared at her, not believing what he saw. Yellow Leaf had the eerie feeling that she was staring into clear water and seeing her reflection. His features were her own. If her longer hair were loose instead of braided, they would look like twins!

"Mother! Come!" the confused boy called urgently. A tall slim woman stepped out of the tepee. Her face too reflected bewilderment as she looked at the girl. She gasped and clutched her throat when she saw the copper medallion Yellow Leaf wore. It was a smaller copy of her own. She moaned and shook her head from side to side. "No . . . It can't be. It's too long ago . . . the soldier said they found her dead . . . "

Although the woman was denying the truth, there was no doubt in Yellow Leaf's mind. The beautiful face was sadder and older but it was the same one she had seen in a hundred dreams and in leaping flames. She would have known her immediately, even without the necklace. She ached to rush to her, but she didn't dare. Panic swept over her. Suppose her mother rejected her! Her yearning for her lost family might be one-sided. For the first time it occurred to her that she might not be loved or wanted!

Thoroughly crushed, Yellow Leaf stood trembling, slow tears trickling down her face. She turned away and blindly groped for the reins. "No! Wait!" Mountain Bird cried, rushing to her. She raised the wet face and stared into Yellow Leaf's brimming eyes. "The face . . . the necklace her father made for her . . . " she whispered, but she still couldn't believe. She took the girl's icy hands and pulled her into the tepee. "Take off your blouse," she said. Mutely Yellow Leaf raised leaden arms and slowly removed it.

"The birthmark. Like a red berry stain. It's there on your shoulder!" Mountain Bird cried. "You *are* Summer Skies. My daughter!" She clasped the weeping girl in her arms and rocked her like an infant. Yellow Leaf sighed deeply and reached up to touch her mother's happy face. The long search had ended.

Yellow Leaf discovered that her memory of two brothers also proved correct. Red Beaver was the first she had met. He was two summers older than her, Mountain Bird said. Another younger brother, Brown Elk, turned up at dusk. The reunited family sat by the cooking fire until almost dawn, asking and answering questions, trying to fit all the pieces of their separate lives together. But it would take many weeks to catch up.

"I feel more like Yellow Leaf, not Summer Skies," she murmured hesitantly to her mother. She was relieved and happy when Mountain Bird smiled and said she too thought she should keep the name her kindly white father had given her. "The drifting golden leaf that fell and named you was an omen. I would not want to go against it. And besides, you are used to the name," the woman said.

"Brown Elk looks like me, but you and Red Beaver look like Tall Trees, your father," Mountain Bird said fondly, holding her daughter's hand in hers.

She read the anxious question in Yellow Leaf's eyes. "Tall Trees is dead," she said bitterly. "His death was so senseless. It happened near the end of the march. Some of the soldiers got drunk one night. They began to shoot — at the stars, the trees, and then at the half-starved masses of misery we had become. We cried out, wept and huddled together, but seven were killed and many wounded before an officer could stop them. Some were children. Tall Trees was shot through the heart — by white jackals not fit to herd rattlesnakes!" she spat, eyes glowing with hatred. "And after surviving so much ∵ . . . so much. Why? Why did he suffer and come all this way just to die and be buried in earth so far from the burial grounds of our people?"

Her children were silent. There was no answer and their mother didn't expect one, but Yellow Leaf shivered with sudden hatred for the white soldiers. She shared her mother's helpless rage. She and her family could never be happy here in this place. Somehow she was going to take them back to the land that had been theirs for centuries, and where there was a freedom of sorts. More, at least, than they had ever known here. And this time they had a goal—Cagle's cabin. If necessary, she would fight, plot, or steal for her family. They were going away from this place of misery and hopelessness. She would camp outside the town and send for the white sheriff. She would sign the paper and get the rest of Cagle's money. She had a family to fight for now. It made her brave.

The family looked frightened as she talked and explained her plans. Hope and freedom to move about the country like settlers were not for Indians to even think about.

"You don't talk or think like an Indian," Red Beaver blurted uneasily.

"Yes, I know," his sister sighed. "That's why I keep getting into trouble. But we are going back before it's too late. I know the whites, and how to deal with them!"

"But we know about white soldiers and rigid government control," Mountain Bird thought, but she remained silent, daring to hope. Could this child help them out of this parched brown land, and back to the green mountains she remembered? She would let her children decide.

A week later Yellow Leaf and Red Beaver traveled to a village she had visited when she first arrived here and bought three wiry Indian ponies from a herd she had seen. Her brother was embarrassed by her fierce haggling, and surprised when she got them for the three large gold coins she had carried with her. She had left the rest of the gold with Mountain Bird. If she had only three she would not be tempted to spend too much and would bargain harder.

Her family did not share Yellow Leaf's optimism, but they were swept along by her determination. Red Beaver had never seen another girl or woman like his sister. She would not consider defeat once she had decided on a course. He would not want such a headstrong wife, but he began to have faith in her. Brown Elk was ready to follow Yellow Leaf anywhere. He had grown up listening to stories about the beautiful ancestral land; he had to see it. His sister could lead them there.

Mountain Bird was willing to go, but she predicted that the soldiers would catch them and bring them back. Because of this they left the tepee standing and slipped away during the night without bidding farewell to anyone in the village. The other Indians would not have to lie. They could not tell what they didn't know. The family was there one night and swallowed up by morning, leaving an empty tepee in the settlement. The exasperated officials would not hear about it for some time. When they did, there would probably be some superstitious story told about the mysterious disappearance.

CHAPTER 13

Her family found that Yellow Leaf was cunning and experienced at eluding whites. They traveled at night and stopped to sleep at dawn. The boys were experts with the bow and arrow, so there were only a few meatless days. When Mountain Bird looked tired, they camped for a few days. This gave Yellow Leaf the opportunity to set snares for extra food. But the delays worried her. Summer was almost gone and they still had so far to go. It was turning colder and they had left too much behind. They needed blankets and other supplies. She was going to have to enter a town!

A few nights later they hit a network of well traveled roads. It was late and there was no traffic, so they made good time. At daylight they set up a camp in dense trees, well off the road. Then Yellow Leaf slipped away to look for the town she knew was nearby. She had passed through this area before with the Schmidt family, but this was not the town where they were taunted and stoned. Instead of riding down the main street, she rode behind the stores and stopped when she saw an elderly man loading flour into a wagon. It was too early for many people to be moving around the town. The man watched her curiously, but without fear or anger.

"I have money and I want to buy some supplies," Yellow Leaf said quietly, holding out some of the small thin gold coins.

"All right," he agreed, "but I don't want my customers getting all churned up at the sight of an Indian. You'll have to wait here. Tell me what you want and I'll bring it." He spoke with an accent that was different from the Schmidts'.

Yellow Leaf nodded with relief. She had no desire to enter. She preferred to shop from outside his store. The man, she noticed, had called her Indian, not "Injun." She ordered blankets, cornmeal, a bag of salt, and other staples. Then she thought of Brown Elk. "Do I have enough for some candy for my little brother — and maybe some red ribbon for my mother?" she asked timidly.

The gray haired man smiled and nodded. "I'll pick some out, and I just got in four spools of new ribbon. I've got a bright red, and some pretty blue grosgrain, if you want some for yourself."

Yellow Leaf hesitated, then shook her head. "Could you hurry please?" she asked tensely. She was trembling and her palms were wet with perspiration.

The man was back in a few minutes and helped her tie the supplies on her horse. He took the gold coins and gave her some silver and copper change, which she hadn't expected. He understood her fear and that she desperately wanted to avoid trouble. "You could follow that line of trees across my land instead of going back along the road," he offered.

Yellow Leaf nodded and thanked him. They had come a long way, but she didn't know how far the Army might search. The man reminded her of Cagle, although they didn't look alike. "What is your name, mister?" she asked.

"Ragan," he said proudly. "James C. Ragan, from county Cork in Ireland. That's clear across the ocean," he added.

The girl mulled over his pride as she entered the trees and took the longer and safer way back to their campsite.

If they were going to adapt to the white man's way of life, her family would need a second name. She repeated the name Ragan several times and liked the sound of it. Her family would adopt that name, she decided, and they would do nothing to shame it.

Her family was shocked when they learned she had actually entered a white town. They had never seen one and preferred not to after the harrowing story of Cagle's death. But Yellow Leaf felt that the risk had been worth it when she handed out her gifts.

Mountain Bird was delighted with the length of sleek red ribbon. Yellow Leaf cut it in half and bound the ends of her thick gray braids and tied bows. They all laughed at their mother's blushes when Red Beaver told her how beautiful she was. The man had been generous in his selection of candy, which Red Beaver and Brown Elk had never tasted before. There was enough for all of them. She gasped when she saw the coil of bright blue ribbon at the bottom of the bag. She was sure the man had not charged her for it. She smoothed it out and noticed that it was grained, like polished wood. She almost wished the man hadn't done it. Every time she decided to hate all white people, she got confused by an unexpected act of kindness. He had given her the ribbon, and his name, although he would never know that.

The sight of the first foothills, covered with thick stands of familiar trees, made Mountain Bird weep with joy. She remembered the names and called them out. For the first time she began to have real hope that they had escaped. Yellow Leaf had assured them that the soldiers no longer gathered up the remaining Indians and forced them west. The small and migrating groups were hardly worth the bother. But Mountain Bird hardly dared believe it. Her daughter had, after all, admitted that some large tribes were confined. All were poor and scorned by white people, even those free to migrate. But they were free so far, although they owned no land and were only tolerated if they stayed away from the white people and their towns.

Mountain Bird would settle for all that. If she could be back in the green mountains where she had been a young and happy wife, she would expect nothing more.

She was certain they would remain poor and homeless, with Yellow Leaf's beloved cabin taken by whites, but she was happy with her reunited family. She worried more, however, about her beautiful daughter. The girl was cunning but too daring, which was dangerous. She was strong willed and relentless in her determination to outwit the white people — their soldiers and even their powerful government! Of necessity she was their leader, and it was she who made all the important decisions, but her mother was full of fear and confusion. Red Beaver was a young brave. He was older and should be the head of the family. It was strange that he admired and trusted his sister and showed no resentment at her leadership. Mountain Bird sighed deeply. It was a changing world. The younger generation was different from hers. She would have to accept it.

Yellow Leaf was on familiar ground now and she pushed them as fast as she dared. The weather was often rainy and cold, so they wore their warm blankets and shared her bed furs. Yellow Leaf worried constantly about illness, or an injury to one of the horses that might delay them further. They had to reach the cabin before the snows came. She and her brothers would set Cagle's traps. The small hoard of gold coins would buy meager supplies for the winter. But the cabin! Was it still there? Was it occupied? She slept restlessly, tortured by nightmares.

She was surprised when they reached the river. It had

shrunk under the hot summer sun. It was half its former width, with wide, sandy beaches on each side. They watched the flatboat from the trees. For the first time her mother and Red Beaver balked. They were afraid and would not approach the white crew. "We have avoided whites all these long miles, and now you want to place us at their mercy!" Mountain Bird cried. "Even if we were allowed to board the boat, they could throw us into the water halfway across. Who would ever know? I want to search for a narrow place where we can ford this river as we have all the others."

"This mighty river is different from all the others. That's why it is called the Father of Waters. There is no narrow place. There's a strong current and undertows. The horses would drown and we would be swept away," Yellow Leaf argued. "Besides, I know this man and how to deal with him. He is not a friend and he won't want to take us, but I can force him to. Please trust me. He will take us!" the girl said imperiously. "You will see."

Mountain Bird turned helplessly to her eldest son. "You are a brave, the head of my family. You make the decision."

Red Beaver looked at Yellow Leaf for a moment. "My sister speaks their language, and she knows about white people. She has done everything she promised, without once failing us. We will follow her," he said. They watched the passengers from the ferry pass their hiding place. No others were waiting on this side to cross over.

"Look! It's that Injun gal again!" one of the crew called out, and pointed. "And this time she's got part of the tribe with her!"

"Hurry! Get aboard, and drag in that gangplank and cast her off!" the owner bawled. "I'll sink it before I'll let 'em on my ferry!"

When she saw the flurry of activity, Yellow Leaf dug

her heels into the horse's flanks and raced ahead of her family. She dropped the reins and leaped off, then jumped across the gap to the end of the boards they were pulling in. The men shook the planks, trying to knock her off, but Yellow Leaf dropped to all fours and catwalked to the deck. "Put the planks back! And tie up so my mother and brothers can ride aboard," she cried breathlessly.

"No! I own this boat and I'll only ferry the passengers I want to take. I ain't takin' you nor any other Injuns across. You kin ford the river or swim, but you won't trick me again!" the ferryman stated flatly. One of the crew had grabbed up one of the long oars. Before she could move out of the way, he hit her with the flat part and knocked her overboard into the shallow water.

The blow enraged Red Beaver so much that he forgot his fear of whites. He put an arrow in his bow and raced the spotted pony along the edge of the water as the crew worked desperately with their oars. Brown Elk followed, also ready to fire. "Don't kill them! Don't kill them!" Yellow Leaf shouted from the muddy water. She knew how expert her brothers were at placing arrows exactly where they aimed, even from the back of a running horse. She envied their skill, and they had promised to teach her.

The youths glanced toward her as she limped out of the river. The blow had been more of a shove, but it had struck her across the thighs. "All right. Don't kill," Red Beaver told his brother grimly, "but place your arrows close!"

The men went white with fear as the first hissing arrow tore a gaping hole in the sleeve of the owner's shirt. It left a long reddening scratch on his bared upper arm. He stood rooted to the deck, afraid he might move in front of the next shot.

The crewman who had struck Yellow Leaf began to

feel like a trussed turkey. He watched an arrow sprout in the wood handle of the oar, smack between his finger and thumb. Blood began to trickle from cuts it gouged out. The next two feathered shafts quivered in the deck, only an inch from the scuffed toes of his boots. He sucked in his breath when the last, shot from Brown Elk's bow, took his wide brimmed hat off his head. It swirled off in the yellowish water, still pierced by the deadly shaft. The boys lowered their bows when the boat pulled out of range.

"We're trapped here now, with no way to cross," Red Beaver sighed hopelessly. He was disappointed in his sister, which he knew wasn't fair after all she had already accomplished. But he thought she had overestimated her cunning this time. He had too. The white men had defeated them and won after all. They always did, he remembered.

"Will we have to go back to the Territory?" Brown Elk asked fearfully.

"No, little brother. We *will* cross here, and on *that* ferry!" Yellow Leaf promised. She was already making new plans. The brothers looked at each other as she wrung muddy water out of her skirt. Dreams and stubbornness were one thing; reality was another. Red Beaver's shoulders slumped as they turned and followed her back to their mother.

Mountain Bird was panic-stricken. Red Beaver and Brown Elk had drawn white blood! Only a little, it was true, but enough to doom them all. They had followed her daughter to disaster. "The soldiers will come now," she croaked. "They will shackle my sons. We will all be taken back and imprisoned as troublemakers. You will never see the white man's cabin again!"

"We aren't beaten yet," Yellow Leaf flashed. "And I have never seen a white soldier. There are none here."

"Oh, yes, my daughter! You have seen them. Many of

112

them," Moutain Bird whispered. "For your own safety, I wish you could remember. The white man did you no favor by raising you with blind and unreasoning courage. You are rash and foolish. Even a young coon knows when it is treed!"

Yellow Leaf led them into the woods without answering. Because her family didn't know what else to do, they followed her instructions. They worked that day and all night, without sleeping. When morning came, there were five bark wigwams standing by the river. Smoke from several cooking fires hung over the camp. When they saw travelers on either side of the river, they moved back and forth and led the horses around, to give the appearance of a larger group. Those who came over the hill retreated in haste when they saw Indians camped at the ferry landing. People on the other shore also left without boarding the moored boat. At noon no crossings had been made.

The family took turns napping while one or two stood guard. "The boat! The boat is coming!" Brown Elk shouted, shaking his sister awake. Yellow Leaf hurried outside the tepee and watched the ferry approach. There were no passengers aboard, just the boat owner and his crew. This encouraged Yellow Leaf. The ferry stopped well off shore and put out several anchors. Her brothers came and stood beside her. They strung arrows in their bows.

"Yore illegally camped at my ferry landing. Yore a'ruinin' my business," the owner shouted angrily. "If you don't pack up and leave, I'm going to send for the U. S. marshal!"

"We're camped on part of the river bed!" Yellow Leaf retorted. "Do you have papers to show you own land that is usually under water? We won't leave. My mother is not going to swim her horse across. We will stay here until you let us on your ferry and take us across!"

"Never! I'll have you removed by force. You attacked me and my men and wounded us with arrows. The law is on our side!" he shouted.

"Your small wounds will be healed before a law man arrives!" Yellow Leaf scoffed. "You and your men tried to drown me. My brothers acted only to defend me. How will you explain that you and your crew were so afraid of me? I won't look like that much danger to a marshal. Taking us across is such a simple thing, and much quicker. I did you a favor before. Of course, I could tell the marshal, your crew, and all your neighbors the truth about our last meeting. Would you prefer that, 'Injun' Zacharia?" she taunted, reminding him of the other crossing and of a fierce war party that didn't exist.

The man turned almost purple with rage. "Yore a filthy redskin squaw! A liar and a cheat!" he choked. Red Beaver didn't understand the words but he knew they were insults. He raised his bow and the man's voice sputtered and trailed off. "Take the savages aboard!" he roared to the sullen crew.

Her frightened family crossed the planks quickly. Red Beaver's restless eyes watched the men as Brown Elk tied the horses to the iron rings as his sister instructed. Mountain Bird sat near her horse, chanting softly, hoping to appease the river demons. Her heart was heavy. Yellow Leaf had taken Red Beaver's bow. She prayed that the men would not move or threaten them. Her daughter was the worst marksman she had ever seen!

Yellow Leaf stayed close behind the owner until her family reached the top of the hill on the other side, then she made him cross the boards with her. The crew pulled in part of the gangplank and cast off at her orders. "Jump

114

for the boat and go on across," she said. The man leaped across the widening gap and slipped in the water to his waist. A crewman pulled him aboard. He cursed and shook his fists in the air. Yellow Leaf leaped on her horse and loped after her family.

Her mother and brothers were subdued as Yellow Leaf led them toward the Tompkins farm. They were still shaken by the experience at the river, and horrified that she had dared defy the group of white men. Not even a warrior would be so foolhardy. What if the bluff had not worked? How had she won? None of them fully understood what had taken place, but she had kept her promise. They had boarded the ferry and crossed safely.

The white family greeted them warmly, delighted to see Yellow Leaf again. The girl had done the impossible. She had made the hazardous journey, found the family whose names she did not know, and returned with them. They hadn't expected to learn the end of her story. Mr. Tompkins, also red-haired like the other members of his family, was courteous but restrained at first, but Jeb and the boys were friends from the start. Even Mountain Bird gradually lost her unease at being around white people when Mrs. Tompkins placed Cagle, a dimpled and gurgling baby now, in her arms. She had never seen a white baby. The two women couldn't understand each other but they shared a common bond. Both were mothers. They smiled at each other and cooed over the baby with flaming hair.

Yellow Leaf's family stayed at the Tompkins farm for two days. Because the house was too small for all to enter, the Indian family camped in the yard. It was good to rest for a few days. The women cooked big meals and the boys fished or hunted. Mrs. Tompkins was pregnant again, so Yellow Leaf searched for fresh herbs to leave her. She dug roots and selected cures for many winter illnesses and tied them to the rafters to dry. Jeb copied the names of the plant parts, the proper dosage and directions as to how they should be prepared for specific illnesses.

Their crops had been laid by and it had been a good year for the white family. Jeb and his father had already made a trip down the river to a town to purchase the winter's supply of staples they could not raise on the farm. After thinking it over, Yellow Leaf hesitantly asked Mr. Tompkins if he would sell them what her family needed. "You are free to enter any town to buy more. It is very risky for us. I know it is much to ask, and you would have to make another trip, but I am willing to pay extra for your trouble."

Mr. Tompkins was happy to accommodate her. He would have offered if he had thought of it. He should have, since his wife and Jeb had told him all about the girl and about Cagle's tragic death. No wonder she was afraid to return to a white town! Besides, he had a lot of admiration for this indomitable Indian girl who refused to be beaten down by his people. And he was in her debt. She had delivered and named his new son and cared for his family when they had no one else to help. It was really a small favor. He and Jeb would enjoy making another trip.

Their horses were heavy-laden as the Indian family traveled the last leg of their journey. Besides selling them what they needed, their white friends had given them seeds for spring planting and a load of dried fruit and fresh vegetables. There was still time to cut firewood and to smoke fish. Yellow Leaf had decided that she and Red Beaver would make a trip to the Indian camp before they broke up and headed south, to buy more grain, pumpkins, and other needs.

She was quiet as she considered the last and biggest worry. The cabin! Would it still be there? Suppose there

117

had been a lightning strike or forest fire. Had squatters moved in? If so, they would not stay! Her name was on Cagle's legal paper. The sheriff was a white man she could trust. He had treated her fairly. He would be able to tell her how to reclaim the cabin and her land, but she hoped it would not be necessary.

She stopped the horse and turned to face her weary family. "Cagle's longest trapline ended there," she said, pointing. Her dark eyes glowed with pride. "You have just crossed onto my land. *Mine!*" She said exultantly. "A white man's paper says it belongs to me, and now it is yours too. This is our home and no one can drive us away!" She galloped away, over the familiar game trail. The horse needed little urging. He seemed to remember it too.

Yellow Leaf was pale and her heart hammered with fear and hope as she approached the clearing. The lake glinted like a jewel through the trees. She topped the slope where Naantam had stood off the renegade Indians and slid off the horse. Tears spilled down her cheeks. She was glad she was alone. How was it possible to be so bone-weary and so happy at the same time?

The clearing was choked with tall stalks of weeds, turning brown, but the beautiful cabin was deserted and exactly as she had left it. A little more weathered perhaps, and with patches of bright green moss growing on the wood shingles. Ivy had crept up the stones of the fireplace. "Oh, Cagle. I love you!" she whispered as she led the horse down toward the faded picture drawing on the front door. She could hear horses coming behind her. Her family. She and her family were home at last.